T0385764

"This series resonates with the priorities of the pulpit. No academic aloofness here, but down-to-earth, preacher-to-preacher meat for God's people."

Bryan Chapell, Pastor Emeritus, Grace Presbyterian Church, Peoria, Illinois

"The single best resource for faithful biblical exposition available today. A great boon for genuine reformation!"

Timothy George, Distinguished Professor of Divinity, Beeson Divinity School, Samford University

"There is a long history of informed, edifying biblical expositions that have been mightily used for God to shape and strengthen the church. These volumes admirably fit this tradition."

D. A. Carson, Cofounder and Theologian-at-Large, The Gospel Coalition

"Throughout the Christian centuries, working pastors have been proving themselves to be the best of all Bible expositors. Kent Hughes stands in this great tradition, and his exciting expositions uphold it worthily."

J. I. Packer, Late Board of Governors' Professor of Theology, Regent College

"The Preaching the Word series is a fine set of commentaries for any pastor. It has a great balance between intellect and heart, covering both interpretation and application. You can't go wrong with this set. It will improve your preaching."

Rick Warren, Pastor, Saddleback Church, Lake Forest, California

"It is a pleasure to commend this series of homiletical commentaries. They fill an enormous vacuum that exists between the practical needs of the pastor/teacher and the critical exegetical depth of most commentaries."

Walter C. Kaiser Jr., President Emeritus and Colman M. Mockler Distinguished Professor Emeritus of Old Testament, Gordon-Conwell Theological Seminary

EZRA,
NEHEMIAH,
AND ESTHER

PREACHING THE WORD
Edited by R. Kent Hughes

Genesis | R. Kent Hughes

Exodus | Philip Graham Ryken

Leviticus | Kenneth A. Mathews

Numbers | Iain M. Duguid

Deuteronomy | Ajith Fernando

Joshua | David Jackman

Judges and Ruth | Barry G. Webb

1 Samuel | John Woodhouse

2 Samuel | John Woodhouse

1 Kings | John Woodhouse

Ezra, Nehemiah, and Esther | Wallace P. Benn

Job | Christopher Ash

Psalms, vol. 1 | James Johnston

Proverbs | Raymond C. Ortlund Jr.

Ecclesiastes | Philip Graham Ryken

Song of Solomon | Douglas Sean O'Donnell

Isaiah | Raymond C. Ortlund Jr.

Jeremiah and Lamentations | R. Kent Hughes

Daniel | Rodney D. Stortz

Matthew | Douglas Sean O'Donnell

Mark | R. Kent Hughes

Luke | R. Kent Hughes

John | R. Kent Hughes

Acts | R. Kent Hughes

Romans | R. Kent Hughes

1 Corinthians | Stephen T. Um

2 Corinthians | R. Kent Hughes

Galatians | Todd Wilson

Ephesians | R. Kent Hughes

Philippians, Colossians, and Philemon | R. Kent Hughes

1–2 Thessalonians | James H. Grant Jr.

1–2 Timothy and Titus | R. Kent Hughes and Bryan Chapell

Hebrews | R. Kent Hughes

James | R. Kent Hughes

1–2 Peter and Jude | David R. Helm

1–3 John | David L. Allen

Revelation | James M. Hamilton Jr.

The Sermon on the Mount | R. Kent Hughes

(((PREACHING *the* WORD)))

EZRA, NEHEMIAH, AND ESTHER

RESTORING *the* CHURCH

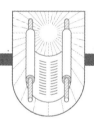

WALLACE P. BENN

R. Kent Hughes
Series Editor

:: CROSSWAY®

WHEATON, ILLINOIS

Library of Congress Cataloging-in-Publication Data

Names: Benn, Wallace P., author. | Hughes, R. Kent, 1942- editor.
Title: Ezra, Nehemiah, and Esther : restoring the church / Wallace P. Benn ; R. Kent Hughes, series editor.
Description: Wheaton, Illinois : Crossway, [2021] | Includes bibliographical references and index.
Identifiers: LCCN 2020054789 (print) | LCCN 2020054790 (ebook) | ISBN 9781433573491 (hardcover) | ISBN 9781433573507 (pdf) | ISBN 9781433573514 (mobi) | ISBN 9781433573521 (epub)
Subjects: LCSH: Bible. Hagiographa—Criticism, interpretation, etc. | Bible. Ezra—Criticism, interpretation, etc. | Bible. Nehemiah—Criticism, interpretation, etc. | Bible. Esther—Criticism, interpretation, etc.
Classification: LCC BS1308 .B47 2021 (print) | LCC BS1308 (ebook) | DDC 222/.06—dc23
LC record available at https://lccn.loc.gov/2020054789
LC ebook record available at https://lccn.loc.gov/2020054790

Crossway is a publishing ministry of Good News Publishers.

VP		30	29	28	27	26	25	24	23	22	21
15	14	13	12	11	10	9	8	7	6	5	4	3	2	1

To Lindsay Jane Benn, my beloved wife of over forty years, without whose love, prayers, help, and encouragement this book would never have been finished.

And in memory of the late Rev. Dr. J. Alec Motyer, who taught me to love the Old Testament as well as the New and encouraged me to preach it as God's Word written.

Restore us again, O God of our salvation,
and put away your indignation toward us!
Will you be angry with us forever?
Will you prolong your anger to all generations?
Will you not revive us again,
that your people may rejoice in you?
*Show us your steadfast love, O L*ORD*,*
and grant us your salvation.

PSALM 85:4–7

Contents

ESTHER

A Word to Those Who
Preach the Word

There are times when I am preaching that I have especially sensed the pleasure of God. I usually become aware of it through the unnatural silence. The ever-present coughing ceases, and the pews stop creaking, bringing an almost physical quiet to the sanctuary—through which my words sail like arrows. I experience a heightened eloquence, so that the cadence and volume of my voice intensify the truth I am preaching.

There is nothing quite like it—the Holy Spirit filling one's sails, the sense of his pleasure, and the awareness that something is happening among one's hearers. This experience is, of course, not unique, for thousands of preachers have similar experiences, even greater ones.

What has happened when this takes place? How do we account for this sense of his smile? The answer for me has come from the ancient rhetorical categories of *logos*, *ethos*, and *pathos*.

The first reason for his smile is the *logos*—in terms of preaching, God's Word. This means that as we stand before God's people to proclaim his Word, we have done our homework. We have exegeted the passage, mined the significance of its words in their context, and applied sound hermeneutical principles in interpreting the text so that we understand what its words meant to its hearers. And it means that we have labored long until we can express in a sentence what the theme of the text is—so that our outline springs from the text. Then our preparation will be such that as we preach, we will not be preaching our own thoughts about God's Word, but God's actual Word, his *logos*. This is fundamental to pleasing him in preaching.

The second element in knowing God's smile in preaching is *ethos*—what you are as a person. There is a danger endemic to preaching, which is having your hands and heart cauterized by holy things. Phillips Brooks illustrated it by the analogy of a train conductor who comes to believe that he has been to the places he announces because of his long and loud heralding of them. And that is why Brooks insisted that preaching must be "the bringing of truth through personality." Though we can never perfectly embody the truth we preach, we must be subject to it, long for it, and make it as much a part of our

11

ethos as possible. As the Puritan William Ames said, "Next to the Scriptures, nothing makes a sermon more to pierce, than when it comes out of the inward affection of the heart without any affectation." When a preacher's *ethos* backs up his *logos*, there will be the pleasure of God.

Last, there is *pathos*—personal passion and conviction. David Hume, the Scottish philosopher and skeptic, was once challenged as he was seen going to hear George Whitefield preach: "I thought you do not believe in the gospel." Hume replied, "I don't, but he does." Just so! When a preacher believes what he preaches, there will be passion. And this belief and requisite passion will know the smile of God.

The pleasure of God is a matter of *logos* (the Word), *ethos* (what you are), and *pathos* (your passion). As you preach the Word may you experience his smile—the Holy Spirit in your sails!

R. Kent Hughes

Preface

When my dear friend Kent Hughes originally asked me to write this preaching commentary, I had loved and benefited from preaching through Nehemiah many times. I had used it too in each new church situation I found myself in to set an agenda for the leadership team by examining where the "walls" of the particular work were built and where they were broken down and needed attention. Always, under God, Nehemiah helped and mobilized us to see what was encouraging and in particular what needed attention and how we could address this by catching a renewed vision for the glory of God and the extension of his kingdom.

I had neglected Ezra, however, and failed to see that really Ezra/Nehemiah is one book with the same heartbeat expressed in slightly different ways. Both are concerned with the restoration of the church in Jerusalem and Judea. Both are energized through prayer and belief in the steadfast promise-keeping nature of the God they worship. Both see that if God's people are to be what God wants them to be, then the Word of God, and obedience to it, must be central for their life and health and for the effectiveness of their God-given mission to be a light to the world. Both men are godly leaders, with somewhat different temperaments, but with the same love and same purpose to see God's name honored afresh as the church is restored according to the promise of God. The two complement one another—Ezra, the priest with a passion to teach and preach God's Word, and Nehemiah, the lay leader whose God-given organizational skills and prayerfulness make spiritual reformation possible. I have since loved preaching through Ezra many times too.

What about the book of Esther, this unusual and brilliantly written dramatic book about "Where is God in a pagan world?" Was he still with his people in pagan Susa? As we shall see, he was with his people, working out his saving purposes for them. This is a wonderful book for believers living in a very secular world who sometimes wonder how they will cope and what God is up to. It is also a wonderful book to teach about the providence of God, a much-neglected doctrine among modern evangelical Christians. I have now preached through Esther many times with delight and profit.

The position canonically and historically of these books written after the exile is also of particular significance to us, as I believe the church in the West is going through a time of exile or judgment because of its manifest unfaithfulness to the gospel and the Word of God. Despite many encouragements, liberal teaching has eroded confidence in the Holy Scriptures, and we are not winning generally against the huge neo-pagan secular and materialistic tide. May God have mercy on us and restore, revive, and bless his people so that our nations may once again be shaken by the power of the gospel to change hearts and transform lives. These three books tell us the kind of people God raises up and uses in bringing reformation and revival and how he brings about the restoration of the church of their time. *Lord, please do it again, and use us to be instruments in your hands!*

But these books only partially fulfill their promise. As three books among the very last books of the Old Testament, the promises of God await the coming of great David's greater Son, the Son of God and the Savior of the world. It is only in him that all the promises of God find their "Yes" (2 Corinthians 1:20). But these books do speak of Jesus, show us our need of him, and encourage us to come to him, remain faithful to him, and rejoice in all the blessings we receive in him. These books are part of God's Word written for our learning, and we neglect them to our great loss.

My grateful thanks to Dr. R. Kent Hughes and all at Crossway for their kindness and patience and for giving me the privilege to write this commentary in the Preaching the Word series.

Wallace P. Benn
Easter 2021

Timelines and Chronology

A. Prophecies Fulfilled

Isaiah 44:28; 2 Chronicles 36:22–23; Jeremiah 25:11; 29:10–14; 31:7; 33:9; Zechariah 4:10

B. Timeline

586 B.C.	538 B.C.	516 B.C.	479 B.C.	458 B.C.	445 B.C.
Fall of Judah	**Decree of Cyrus**	**Temple Rebuilt**	**Esther as Queen**	**Ezra Arrives in Jerusalem**	**Nehemiah Arrives in Jerusalem**
Temple destroyed	End of Exile				
Jeremiah/Ezekiel	*Daniel?*	*Haggai/Zechariah*	*Esther*	*Ezra 7–10*	*Nehemiah*

C. Chronology

Chronology of Ezra

Event	Year	Reference
Cyrus king of Persia captures Babylon	539 B.C.	Dan. 5:30–31
First year of King Cyrus; issues proclamation freeing Jewish exiles to return	538–537	Ezra 1:1–4
Jewish exiles, led by Sheshbazzar, return from Babylon to Jerusalem	537?	Ezra 1:11
Altar rebuilt	537	Ezra 3:1–2
Temple rebuilding begins	536	Ezra 3:8
Adversaries oppose the rebuilding	536–530	Ezra 4:1–5
Temple rebuilding ceases	530–520	Ezra 4:24
Temple rebuilding resumes (2nd year of Darius)	520	Ezra 5:2; compare Hag. 1:14
Temple construction completed (6th year of Darius)	516	Ezra 6:15
Ezra departs from Babylon to Jerusalem (arrives in 7th year of Artaxerxes)	458	Ezra 7:6–9
Men of Judah and Benjamin assemble at Jerusalem	458	Ezra 10:9
Officials conduct three-month investigation	458–457	Ezra 10:16–17

Chronology of Nehemiah

Event	Month/Day	Year	Reference
Hanani brings Nehemiah a report from Jerusalem (20th year of Artaxerxes I)		445–444 B.C.	1:1
Nehemiah before King Artaxerxes	1	445	2:1
Nehemiah arrives to inspect Jerusalem walls		445	2:11
Wall is finished	6/25	445	6:15
People of Israel gather	7	445	7:73—8:1
People of Israel celebrate Feast of Booths	7/15–22	445	8:14
People of Israel fast and confess sins	7/24	445	9:1
Nehemiah returns to Susa (32nd year of Artaxerxes I)		433	5:14; 13:6

Taken from page 652 of the ESV® Global Study Bible™ (The Holy Bible, English Standard Version®), copyright © 2012 by Crossway, a publishing ministry of Good News Publishers. Used by permission. All rights reserved.

Chronology in Esther

Reference	Event	Month	Day	Year of Ahasuerus's Reign	Year
1:3	Ahasuerus holds his banquets			3	483 B.C.
2:16	Esther goes to Ahasuerus	10		7	479
3:7	Haman casts his lots	1		12	474
3:12	Haman issues his decree	1	13	12	474
3:13	Date planned for annihilation of the Jews	12	13	13	473
8:9	Mordecai issues his decree	3	23	13	473
8:12; 9:1	Day upon which Jews could defend themselves from attack	12	13	13	473
9:6-10, 20-22	Ten sons of Haman executed; Feast of Purim celebrated	12	14, 15	13	473

Taken from page 677 of the ESV® Global Study Bible™ (The Holy Bible, English Standard Version®), copyright © 2012 by Crossway, a publishing ministry of Good News Publishers. Used by permission. All rights reserved.

D. Postexilic Returns to Jerusalem

Sequence	Date	Scripture	Jewish Leader	Persian Ruler
First	538 B.C.	Ezra 1—6	Zerubbabel, Joshua	Cyrus
Second	458 B.C.	Ezra 7—10	Ezra	Artaxerxes
Third	445 B.C.	Nehemiah 1—13	Nehemiah	Artaxerxes

EZRA

The Timeline of Ezra

586 B.C.	**538** B.C.	**516** B.C.	**458** B.C.
Fall of Judah/	Decree of Cyrus/	Temple Rebuilt	Ezra Arrives
Temple Destroyed	End of Exile		in Jerusalem

1

Our God Reigns—See God

EZRA 1

WHY STUDY EZRA? Because it is a neglected part of God's Word written, and no part of the Holy Scriptures should be neglected. Bruce Waltke talks about it in his excellent *Old Testament Theology* as "a story the church needs to hear but rarely does."[1] It is the story of a second exodus as God's people return from seventy years of captivity in Persia, and after a period of judgment it is a story of grace, forgiveness, and restoration. It is a story of new beginnings and a period of church reviving.

In a powerful and beautiful passage, Ezra (9:6–9) describes what has been going on. He confesses the sin of the professing church of his day (the people of Judah, the Jews), which has been the cause of the terrible events of 586 B.C. when Jerusalem and its temple were destroyed by Nebuchadnezzar and the last portion of the people were taken into exile. But now in grace and mercy, and in fulfillment of his promise, God is reviving, restoring, and bringing the people home. It is a time of "a little reviving in our slavery" when God has shown his steadfast love for his people and his willingness "to grant us some reviving to set up the house of our God, to repair its ruins, and to give us protection in Judea and Jerusalem" (9:8–9). Ezra describes a time of church revival and restoration after a period of difficulty and judgment.

Back in the 1980s, J. I. Packer suggested that the church in the West was going through a period of judgment for its manifold disobedience and unfaithfulness to God's Word. I trust you come from a church situation that is encouraging, seeing growth, and knowing God's blessing, but it is certainly true that despite many encouraging signs the church in the Western world (unlike the church elsewhere) is not winning overall against the huge secular, unbelieving, materialistic tide it is facing. I remember a bishop from Africa telling me in 1998 that more people were becoming Christians in his diocese than were being born! That's hugely encouraging, and we in the West need to realize how well the church is doing in the Two-Thirds World, often even in the face of extreme difficulty and persecution. We need that reviving too! The old mainstream Protestant denominations are riven with disagreement between those who want to be faithful to the Scriptures and those who simply wish to be in tune with the values of our time whatever the cost. We need God to revive and restore us, bringing us back to joy in the gospel of grace and the abiding truths of the Bible as the crucial answer to our deepest needs before God. On a more personal note, which one of us reading this text is as obedient to God's Word as we should be or takes with wisdom and courage all the opportunities God gives us to live and witness for him? We need reviving too, so that in a fresh way we may be the people God wants us to be. So Ezra is deeply relevant.

The books of Ezra and Nehemiah were originally one, and they need to be read, studied, and ideally preached together. They cover three returns of God's people to the land. The first and main one in 538 B.C. included the building of the second temple (Solomon's temple being the first, destroyed in 586 B.C.), which was finished in 516 B.C. (see Ezra 1—6). The second return was in 458 B.C. with Ezra himself leading a group (see Ezra 7—10). The third return to Jerusalem was in 445 B.C. under the leadership of Nehemiah. This period covered the reign of four Persian kings (Cyrus, Darius, Xerxes, and Artaxerxes) and covers approximately the last 100 years or so of Old Testament history (see the earlier chart). It was a period of God's blessing and faithfulness despite continuing sin among the people, but a time that looked forward to what God would do to bless and restore his people with the coming of the messianic king, the Lord Jesus Christ.

Ezra shows us how God goes about blessing and reviving his people. If we are to know his reviving touch, we should ask God to do the same fundamental things among us as he did among his people then. What is the first step in God reviving his people? It is to renew their vision of his sovereign power and covenant faithfulness.

Ezra 1 follows directly from the previous book (2 Chronicles 36:22–23) and tells us that God's Word can be trusted because God keeps his promises. The decree of Cyrus is the direct result of the fullfillment of prophecies that were stated long before. See the remarkable mention of Cyrus by name in Isaiah 44:28:

> who says of Cyrus, "He is my shepherd,
>   and he shall fulfill all my purpose";

saying of Jerusalem, "She shall be built,"
and of the temple, "Your foundation shall be laid."

Josephus, the Jewish historian, speculated that Cyrus—when shown this prophecy or when reading it himself—was then prompted by it to take action. Be that as it may, Ezra says it was really God who stirred him to issue this decree (1:1).

Note also the specific prophecy mentioned by Ezra that is being fulfilled—Jeremiah 29:10–14:

> For thus says the Lord: When seventy years are completed for Babylon, I will visit you, and I will fulfill to you my promise and bring you back to this place. For I know the plans I have for you, declares the Lord, plans for welfare and not evil, to give you a future and a hope. Then you will call upon me and come and pray to me, and I will hear you. You will seek me and find me, when you seek me with all your heart. I will be found by you, declares the Lord, and I will restore your fortunes and gather you from all the nations and all the places where I have driven you, declares the Lord, and I will bring you back to the place from which I sent you into exile.

This was now happening, said Ezra. (See also Jeremiah 25:11; 31:7–8; 33:9; Zechariah 4:10.)

Redeeming and Restoring His People

God keeps his covenant promises to his people, and his word of promise can be trusted now as then. Ezra was telling the story of God's redeeming and restoring his people to praise his name and bear witness to him in the world of his day.

The book of Ezra is a story of God's grace and mercy that displays his steadfast love for his people as he refuses to give up on them.

Working through Human History to Achieve His Purpose

If you were a Judean slave in Persia, the superpower of the day, you might have wondered how on earth you would ever get back to Jerusalem. Perhaps there would be a coup and you could escape. Unlikely, given Cyrus's power. Maybe someone would poison the king and in the ensuing chaos you could slip away. That was not the way God did it at all. Instead in a peaceful way he "stirred up the spirit of Cyrus" (1:1) to issue the decree recorded in verses 2–4.

This is remarkable in many ways, and the way it is phrased in Ezra 1 shows a clear respect for "the God of heaven." This was a smart political move on Cyrus's part, and though of particular benefit to the people of Judea in exile, we know from The Cyrus Cylinder (a renowned document in the British Museum) that such a decree was extended to many other ethnic and religious groups as well. In the vast empire that Cyrus had conquered and sought to control, there were many ethnic groups that had been exiled and displaced. Sending them back on a mission to restore their places of worship would hopefully create a thankful and loyal population throughout his empire. Cyrus was, it seems, a polytheist (note the phrase "may his God be with him," v. 3) and a worshiper of Marduk. The decree as recorded by Ezra was in a form amenable to the Jewish exiles, but unknown to Cyrus, it was all for their benefit under the sovereign hand of their God.

There is a key lesson to be learned here. In our unstable world of superpowers and wars and rumors of wars, it is not Joe Biden or Vladimir Putin or anyone else who is in control—it is God. His purposes to save, bless, and keep a people for his glory cannot and will not be thwarted. Our God reigns, and he works throughout history and even uses unbelievers to achieve his purposes. If he can use Cyrus, he can use anybody. He rules and overrules the course of human history for his ends. How tremendously encouraging it must have been to a humanly insignificant and captive people to know that their destiny was in safe hands and that God had the power to keep his promises and accomplish all his plans for the good and blessing of his people. In the Western world today, when Christians are often marginalized and seem powerless to stop the neo-pagan tide, how encouraging it is to know that our God still reigns and works out his purposes. My old college principal, mentor, and friend J. Alec Motyer used to say, "The sovereignty of God is the pillow on which I lay my head at night." That has been my and my family's joyful experience for many years now.

Energizing, Stirring Up, and Motivating His People to Do His Will (for Their Joy)

The renewed vision of God's grace and power was the key ingredient in stirring up the people to passionately obey God and trust his promises. The same God that stirred Cyrus stirred the peoples' hearts too. God was at work motivating and energizing them to get up and go (1:5), and it seems that the leaders took the initiative in this. The motivation to obey the Lord, trust his promises, and take the opportunity provided by Cyrus's amazing decree in God's good providence is the precursor to blessing. Obedience is always the way to God's blessing, and it is God's blessing that brings joy.

Providentially Providing for His People in Unexpected Ways

Cyrus suggested that the people of God who stayed behind should support those who were going with needful gifts given generously (1:4, 6). Many commentators suggest, I think rightly, that this included helpful gifts from pagan neighbors as well as believers. This amazing activity shows God behind the event and mirrors what happened in the first exodus (see Exodus 12:35–36).

Even more extraordinary than this, Cyrus commanded that all the vessels taken in plunder by Nebuchadnezzar should be returned (Ezra 1:7). This amounted to a large number of pots and pans, including 5,400 vessels of gold and silver (1:11). There were no statues or idols of any kind since they were forbidden in temple worship. The treasurer in charge of the handover gave them all to the safekeeping of Sheshbazzar, "the prince of Judah," of the royal line of David (1:8), a key figure at this point.

God was showing extreme restorative generosity to his people, who would set out laden with gifts and returned treasure. Anyone who knows the stories of battles by various countries to get the British Museum to return treasures taken in conquest during the days of the British Empire will not fail to be amazed at this provision. The people were setting off on a difficult journey, but they were encouraged by God's gracious providence and provision for them. They must have had a song in their hearts as well as being excited and probably also somewhat nervous about what lay ahead of them. The God who keeps his promises would not fail them now!

New Testament Perspective

It is important that we see the significance of these truths for us as worked out in the New Testament. All these things were written for our learning, and often Old Testament stories reveal truth further displayed and developed in the New Testament.

In Paul's magnificent vision of all that we as believers have in the risen Christ because of his substitutionary death and bodily resurrection and ascension, he prays that Christians may see:

> . . . what is the immeasurable greatness of his power toward us who believe, according to the working of his great might that he worked in Christ when he raised him from the dead and seated him at his right hand in the heavenly places, far above all rule and authority and power and dominion, and above every name that is named, not only in this age but also in the one to come. And he put all things under his feet and gave him as head over all things to the church, which is his body, the fullness of him who fills all in all. (Ephesians 1:19–23)

Notice the phrase describing Christ "as head over all things to [or perhaps more helpfully, "for"] the church." Christ's sovereign authority and power is for the benefit of the church, and he exercises his authority to save, keep, bless, and bring to glory his redeemed people. God's providential care and sovereignty are exercised through history for the glory of his name and the benefit of his people. So Paul can elsewhere say that "for those who love God all things work together for good" (Romans 8:28). Our God reigns, and he reigns in grace and love, working out his purposes for us if we belong to him.

When we have felt stirred to serve our Lord and seek to do his will, it is not our own strength that has so moved us. God has enabled us to so respond; so we should give him the praise. Listen again to Paul:

> Therefore, my beloved, as you have always obeyed, so now, not only as in my presence but much more in my absence, work out your own salvation with fear and trembling, for it is God who works in you, both to will and to work for his good pleasure. (Philippians 2:12–13)

We need to respond to and obey God with all our hearts, but it is God who enables us to do that. As in the days of Ezra, so it is now.

Though the nations rage,
Kingdoms rise and fall,
There is still one King
Reigning over all.
So I will not fear for this truth remains:
That my God is the Ancient of Days.

None above Him, none before Him,
All of time in His hands.
For His throne it shall remain and ever stand.
All the power, all the glory,
I will trust in His name;
For my God is the Ancient of Days.

—Jonny Robinson, Rich Thompson, Michael Ray Farren, and Jesse Reeves[*]

[*] Extract taken from the song "Ancient of Days" by Jonny Robinson, Rich Thompson, Michael Farren, and Jesse Reeves. Copyright © 2018 CityAlight Music/Integrity's Alleluia! Music/Farren Love & War (Adm. by CapitolCMGPublishing.com excl. UK & Europe, adm. at IntegrityRights. com)/BECWorship/WriterwrongMusic (Admin by Song Solutions); and © 2018 BEC WORSHIP (ASCAP / Writerwrong Music (ASCAP) (Administered by Music Services) CityAlight Music (Admin. by Capitol CMG Publishing (Integrity Music, David C Cook)) / Farren Love & War Publishing (Admin. by Capitol CMG Publishing (Integrity Music, David C Cook)) / Integrity's Alleluia! Music (Admin. by Capitol CMG Publishing (Integrity Music, David C Cook)).

2

The Church Family Matters—See the Church

EZRA 2

WHO AM I? Where do I belong? These questions are of considerable importance in knowing our identity and our place in the scheme of things.

If you were to ask a Jew (someone who came from Judea originally) in Ezra's time what their identity was, they would say, "I belong to the people of God. That is who I am. The great and true God YHWH has chosen a people for his own possession and glory to bring his light to the world, and I belong to that people. This God has entered into a covenant relationship with us, and we belong to him, though our sin has caused our exile."

Ezra 2 is all about the identity of the people of God—who they really were and what defined them. There can be no blurred edges, as we shall see; no uncertainties about belonging or not, because for these people, all their future hopes were wrapped up in their identity. More than anything else, their identity depended on their relationship with God.

King David beautifully wrote and sang of his experience with God. In the challenging circumstances of being a shepherd boy caring for his sheep in lonely and difficult circumstances, he had proved the reality of God as the shepherd who cared for, protected, and provided for him. The returning exiles in Ezra 2 were experiencing the same grace-filled commitment and care of their shepherd God as the Lord clearly supervised, enabled, protected, and provided for them as they returned to a devastated country with a job to do.

The Good Shepherd Delivers, Restores, and Leads Home

God was delivering them out of the captivity that their sin and disobedience had caused them (2:1). They were coming home, and it was the grace of God that was accomplishing this. Against all human odds, God had turned the heart of the king to enable them to go home, encourage the support of the community in their doing so, and provide for them on that long and hazardous journey, probably taking about four months. God had also stirred the people's hearts to respond to God's initiative and take up the challenge of the journey and the challenges they would face when they got there (1:1, 5).

Notice that they returned under the leadership of "the heads of the fathers' houses" (1:5) that expanded to twelve men (2:2; 1:8 adds Sheshbazzar, making him the twelfth). The twelve leaders represent the twelve tribes of the ancient people of God. Israel was once again being reconstituted, restored to what it once was. God had kept his promise, had not given up on them, and was taking them home once again.

The Good Shepherd Knows His Sheep by Name

Have you ever wondered why all the lists in the Bible are there, giving so many names otherwise long forgotten and so difficult to read aloud in church? If you belong to God by grace and faith, you may never be famous or make it into a secular world history of significant people, but you will not be forgotten by God or be anything other than significant in his sight. So how good it is to see this list of names; in New Testament terms, if we are disciples of Christ, how good it is to know that our names are written in "the Lamb's book of life" (Revelation 21:27).

The Good Shepherd Cares about His Sheep (and Their Lambs)

The list is especially important here in the reconstitution of the people of God. It tells us who they were and how many they were. It defines and sets boundaries. The list also shows that families matter to God ("sons of" is repeated throughout the chapter). Passing on the faith in our families matters to God also. Many years earlier, God had promised Abraham that his offspring would be as innumerable as the stars and that one of his offspring would bring blessing to all the nations of the world (Genesis 15:5). Humanly speaking, that depended on Abraham's descendants keeping their faith and identity. It was from the people of Abraham that one day the Messiah would come (Matthew 1:1–2). So the people of God keeping their identity as recorded here and passing on their faith was of great importance to the purposes of God in their entirety and to the fulfillment of his promises, which they knew would not fail.

It is not surprising that the God who invented marriage for one man and one woman as the context for sexual activity and the multiplication of the human race loves to work in families that seek to honor him. Passing on our faith to our children is of crucial importance in every generation. Parents have a unique and special responsibility in this.

The Good Shepherd Calls His Sheep to Holiness of Life

No uncertainty about belonging could be allowed (2:59). Clarity was needed as to whether a person belonged or not. There could be no fence-sitting! No priest, if there was uncertainty because of intermarriage outside of God's people, could operate until guidance was sought (2:61–63). How this guidance exactly worked at the time remains something of a mystery to us. God's people were to be a holy people set apart for himself and seeking to follow his Word and rule as his redeemed people. There could no compromise about that clarity of desire and commitment.

The Good Shepherd Knows His Sheep Need
Good Leaders to Lead Them in Worship

We see this particularly in 2:2–68. Notice the large numbers of priests and temple servants despite relatively few Levites. They make up approximately one tenth of the total number. This is significant. The people knew they were going back to rebuild the temple and restore worship, and that priority commitment was reflected in these numbers. They would need the help of the priests, temple servants, and Levites.

Also note how some of the other leaders were great examples in showing that worship is the expression of a surrendered life—they gave generously, beyond a tithe (or tenth) (2:68). We all need good examples to lead us in the right direction, and leaders have a particular responsibility to take that seriously.

It is important to note that the overall number of returnees was not huge, approximately 50,000 people. Various estimates of what might have been expected differ, but a realistic and relatively conservative number would probably have been double that amount. Some were perhaps too old and sick to travel. Others had put their roots down in Babylonia and were just too comfortable to move or were not prepared for the spiritual challenge of the journey and the difficult and dangerous task of resettling Judea. "A similar choice repeatedly confronts us as Christians [cf. Hebrews 11:8–27], and may form a test between nominal and real believers. God does not always call us to security."[1]

There was work to be done. There were promises yet to be fulfilled. They needed to settle the land, build the temple, and be obedient to God's ways, which are always the best ways in the long run. To fulfill their calling, they needed one another's support, encouragement, and help and to look to God in each new opportunity and challenge.

New Testament Perspective

First Corinthians 3:16–17 reminds us that in new covenant times, Christians gathering together are the Church of Jesus Christ, the new temple: "God's temple is holy, and you [plural] are that temple." Collectively as the Body of Christ, we are set apart for our Savior's glory, to love and serve him who has loved us so.

First Corinthians 6:19–20 reminds us that individually, if we have invited Jesus to be our Savior and Lord, we are indwelt by the Holy Spirit and are therefore God's temple: "Do you not know that your body is a temple of the Holy Spirit within you, whom you have from God? You are not your own, for you were bought with a price. So glorify God in your body."

Both these truths are very important and need to be held together. We have been saved by grace individually, but then were brought into God's family, the Church. Now we need one another's help and encouragement to live for our Savior and bring glory to him.

Ephesians is the great New Testament book about the doctrine of the Church. Three great pictures of the Church are given us there:

- *The bride of Christ* (Ephesians 5:23–25)—we are loved and are called to respond with love.
- *The body of Christ* (Ephesians 1:22–23; 3:6; 4:4, 12, 15–16; 5:23, 30)— a wonderful picture of our Savior's ownership of us and his intimacy with us and a call to each one of us as part of that Body, gifted and enabled by the Spirit, to play our part in serving Christ and one another (see 1 Corinthians 12—14).
- *The building (temple) of Christ* (Ephesians 2:20–21)—in which Christ is the cornerstone and we are being built together to bring glory to God. This is a call for the Church to grow as the number of the redeemed increases until that great day when our Savior returns. In the meantime we are not to neglect gathering together to encourage, support, and challenge each other to persevere in running the race of faith, looking always to Jesus (Hebrews 10:22–25; 12:1–2).

We need to see the Church afresh and its importance in the purposes of God. We need to play our part in this glorious household/family of God (Ephesians 2:19) to which we are privileged to belong because of the blood of our Savior who died for us as our sin-bearer to restore our relationship with God and enable us to be his children.

We also need to remember that our essential identity comes not from our ethnicity, class, education, possessions, or sexuality but from being in Christ, united to him, and part of God's wonderful family, the Church of Jesus Christ, that unites people from every race, background, and culture.

> In Christ alone my hope is found,
> He is my light, my strength, my song;
> This Cornerstone, this solid Ground,
> Firm through the fiercest drought and storm.
> What heights of love, what depths of peace,
> When fears are stilled, when strivings cease!
> My Comforter, my All in All,
> Here in the love of Christ I stand.
>
> —*Keith Getty and Stuart Townend**

3

First Things First—
Returning to Worship

EZRA 3

IN THE COUNTY IN England where I live, Northamptonshire, there are many little villages built of attractive cream-colored stone. The outstanding building in these villages is the local church, of which there are many fine examples. While it is true that some may have been built for unworthy reasons—perhaps because the local squire wanted to sponsor a better building than another nearby village or town—nonetheless the most important building in all these villages is the church. That says something about the priorities of these village inhabitants in the past. They knew their need of God and their dependence on him to survive and thrive; so the best buildings they built were churches.

When the exiles returned to Jerusalem, they built the altar and then the temple in light of God's earlier promise to them in Exodus 29:42–46:

> It shall be a regular burnt offering throughout your generations at the entrance of the tent of meeting before the LORD, where I will meet with you, to speak to you there. There I will meet with the people of Israel, and it shall be sanctified by my glory. I will consecrate the tent of meeting and the altar. Aaron also and his sons I will consecrate to serve me as priests. I will dwell among the people of Israel and will be their God. And they shall know that I am the LORD their God, who brought them out of the land of Egypt that I might dwell among them. I am the LORD their God.

They were all aware of their need of God's help and protection. So in Ezra 3:3 we read, "They set the altar in its place, for fear was on them because of the peoples of the lands, and they offered burnt offerings on it to the LORD, burnt offerings morning and evening." There was no self-reliant arrogance. They faced the huge task of reclaiming their land and livelihoods and resettling the land. But their primary reason in returning was to rebuild the temple. The temple was the symbol of God's presence among them and with them and what made them the distinct people that they were. How they needed the help and presence of their Lord!

They also understood that a restored relationship with the Lord would come only through the altar and its sacrifices. Their sin created a barrier between them and God's holiness that could only be dealt with by a substitutionary sacrifice. They deserved his judgment, but in grace he provided a way of escape by the sacrificial system and the essential sacrifice of a lamb without blemish at Passover time. They were learning what the New Testament makes clear: "without the shedding of blood there is no forgiveness of sins" (Hebrews 9:22).

So the very first thing they built was an altar, and then they began the cycle of regular sacrifices (Ezra 3:4–5). Their first sacrifices were "burnt offerings" that, though not mandated by Levitical law, were freewill expressions of their unreserved surrender and total devotion to the Lord. Their joy in God's presence with them and his help to them started with God's gracious forgiveness of their sins (which had caused the exile) and all that kept them from a relationship with him.

Let us then spell out what this chapter shows us very clearly.

Laying Spiritual Foundations as Well as Physical Ones (3:11)

Their gratitude to God, surrender to him, and dependence on him expressed itself in joyful worship, stating in music and song all that God's covenant love for them (*hesed*) meant to them. Without it they were nothing and nobodies.

Nothing is more important in our lives than to worship and serve the living God. As a "kingdom of priests" (Exodus 19:6), that was true of God's people then also. So on the seventh month, a significant month in their yearly liturgical calendar, they gathered together as one under the godly leadership of Jeshua the priest, and Zerubbabel, apparently their governor. They built an altar, initiated the sacrificial system, and celebrated the Feast of Booths (3:4), a joyful celebration of God's provision for his people during the wilderness years after their deliverance from Egypt. This new exodus that they had experienced evoked the memory of God's care for them down the generations to that very day.

They were united in their desire to obey the Lord's commands and to worship him in a Biblical way (as written in the Law of Moses, 3:2 and as King David had directed, 3:10). The refrain in verse 11 is found in a number of Psalms (e.g., 136:1–3; 118:1–4) as well as in other places in the Old Testament (e.g., 1 Chronicles 16:34). Maybe other psalms came to mind as well as the temple foundation was laid. For example:

> Oh come, let us sing to the Lord;
>   let us make a joyful noise to the rock of our salvation!
> Let us come into his presence with thanksgiving;
>   let us make a joyful noise to him with songs of praise!
> For the Lord is a great God,
>   and a great King above all gods. . . .
>
> Oh come, let us worship and bow down;
>   let us kneel before the Lord, our Maker!
> For he is our God,
>   and we are the people of his pasture,
>   and the sheep of his hand. (Psalm 95:1–3, 6–7)

Though the altar was built in 537 B.C. after their arrival and initial settling, it took longer to build the temple foundations (3:6). But in the second year of their being back in the land, the work began (536 B.C., 3:8). When the builders laid the foundation, the event was marked by a great service of praise and thanksgiving to the Lord, which included everyone playing their part (3:10–13). So important spiritual foundations were being laid as they began building the physical temple.

The Significance and Symbolism of the Temple
Speaking of God's Presence and Promise

I love the title of Gordon Fee's book on the Holy Spirit—*God's Empowering Presence*. That title wonderfully describes the importance of the temple's symbolism for God's people in Ezra's time, for the temple spoke of God's immanence as well as his transcendence and that he had initiated a relationship by grace with his people and that he, by his presence, dwelt with them and among them. Therein lay their hope of defeating their enemies and knowing God's *shalom*—his peace and the fulfillment of his purposes of grace for them. In human terms, they were small and weak in comparison to other nations, but the greatness they had experienced in national life was God's doing and evidence of his presence with them. He made them great and a light to other nations.

Sacrifice as God's Means of Forgiveness

The way into the presence of God, the Holy of Holies in the temple, was through an altar and the whole sacrificial system of bloody animal sacrifices repeated regularly, with the yearly culmination in the Day of Atonement sacrificial ritual. This drummed into their thinking that atonement for their sin was necessary. Their God was holy and without sin, and if a sinful people were to have a meaningful relationship with him, the price of their sin needed to be paid. As the New Testament makes clear, "the wages of sin is death" (Romans 6:23). The price had to be paid by them or by a substitute sacrificed in their place. If sin was not punished, God was unjust and not holy, and there was no hope of justice in this world (or the next).

But they also knew that their God was supremely a God of covenant grace and mercy who both loved and longed to forgive them. But the sacrificial system showed that this was no cheap grace; it was a costly matter. Their experience in exile had taught them how costly sin and rebellion were. Their persistent unrepented sin and disobedience to God's Word had cost them dearly, and in this new opportunity they needed to know they were on the right footing with God. They needed to avail themselves of and rejoice in God's forgiveness and grace in bringing them home.

Songs of Praise: The Language of Faith

The scene pictured for us in verses 10–13 is one of exuberant praise and worship as the temple foundation was laid. The priests and Levites along with the musicians and singers led the people in praise. Central to their praise was the celebration of God's covenant love for them, which "endures forever" (3:11).

A friend who had no experience of church or the Christian faith came with me to church recently. I asked him afterward what he made of it. "You Christians sing a lot," he said. I replied, "God has put a new song in our hearts because of his love shown to us in Jesus Christ and his sacrificial, substitutionary death on our behalf." Throughout history Christians have sung God's praises. Here in the book of Ezra, God's people are seen doing the same.

My daughter gave me a beautiful plaque one Christmas with the following verse on it, which I read every morning on the wall in my study: "Satisfy us in the morning with your unfailing love, that we may sing for joy and be glad all our days" (Psalm 90:14 NIV). That ought to be true for us if we belong to the Lord, even when days are difficult (cf. Psalm 90:15). There is always a reason for the believer to rejoice.

There is an interesting description not only of joy but also of sorrow in Ezra 3:12–13. While many were joyful, some older people who had survived the exile and remembered the old temple wept because this new one was never going to be as grand or glorious as Solomon's temple had been. This shows us something we will see clearly later on: the nation returning from exile was never as great nor the rebuilt temple as glorious as it had been previously. This last period of Old Testament history leaves us wanting God to do more, and he did. He was preparing his people for the coming of his Son in the fullness of time to walk on the temple mount among us and to be the supreme sacrifice for our sins.

There is perhaps another lesson here to be learned in church life. It is easy for older believers to sometimes unhelpfully compare a present church activity to what happened "in my day." Numbers may have been greater then, but we need to celebrate what God is doing now among his people, not just look back wistfully, which can be so discouraging to a new generation. They needed to heed the Word of the Lord through Zechariah, recorded in Zechariah 4:9–10:

> The hands of Zerubbabel have laid the foundation of this house; his hands shall also complete it. Then you will know that the LORD of hosts has sent me to you. For whoever has despised the day of small things shall rejoice, and shall see the plumb line in the hand of Zerubbabel.

Their practical building was to be the facilitation of their spiritual values and priorities. What they were building was in order to be obedient to God's will for them and to express their faith and the priority values of their lives as God's people.

There is a lesson here for any building program embarked on by a local church congregation. Such a program needs to facilitate our life and worship as God's people and is to be of use in our central calling, which is to bring the gospel to our part of God's world. Our buildings must express our priorities rather than becoming more important than our mission and shaping our priorities. I think of a beautifully built church hall that is not usable for children's work because people are afraid the lovely walls will be spoiled by the dirty hands of children. That is getting things the wrong way around!

Haggai and Zecharia were prophets sent by God at this time (around 520 B.C.) to challenge and encourage the people in the building process. The temple foundation was laid and the building started in 536 B.C., but as we will see in the next chapter, opposition mounted against the building and the work was delayed for ten years (530–520 B.C.). God sent the two prophets to get things moving again, and Haggai especially upbraided the people for letting the pressure get to them and having the wrong priorities.

Four times in two chapters he called on the people to "consider" (Haggai 1:5, 7; 2:15, 18).

> Is it a time for you yourselves to dwell in your paneled houses, while this house lies in ruins? Now, therefore, thus says the LORD of hosts: Consider your ways. You have sown much, and harvested little. You eat, but you never have enough; you drink, but you never have your fill. You clothe yourselves, but no one is warm. And he who earns wages does so to put them into a bag with holes. (Haggai 1:4–6)

They were suffering economically because they had let their priorities slip. They had come back to build God's house, and now they were concentrating on making their own properties impressively fashionable. Early good intentions can easily slip.

But God encouraged his people through Haggai as well: "Be strong, all you people of the land, declares the LORD. Work, for I am with you, declares the LORD of hosts, according to the covenant that I made with you when you came out of Egypt. My Spirit remains in your midst. Fear not" (Haggai 2:4–5). The Lord also promised, "The latter glory of this house shall be greater than the former, says the LORD of hosts. And in this place I will give peace, declares the LORD of hosts" (Haggai 2:9).

This was fulfilled gloriously when the Lord Jesus walked through the temple portals and brought us peace by his death on the cross as our sin-bearer and substitute, rising in triumph over death.

> Bearing shame and scoffing rude,
> In my place condemned he stood;
> Sealed my pardon with His blood;
> Hallelujah! What a Saviour!
>
> —Philip Paul Bliss[1]

New Testament Perspectives

Romans 12:1–2 makes it abundantly clear that worship in new covenant times is no longer temple worship, nor is it an hour or two a week, but rather a surrendered life, continually serving the Lord and giving him his rightful place in our lives as our Savior and Lord. That is our "spiritual worship," and it is, as the phrase can also be translated, "your rational service" (see ESV footnote). That is our only reasonable response to all that God has done for us in Christ.

Praising God daily for his love to us should be a focus of that surrendered life, as should our meeting together on the Lord's Day to praise, pray, and learn together from God's Word and to encourage each other to go on living a life of obedient surrender to the Lord. In the recent rediscovery that worship is about the whole of our lives, it has become a habit by some not to see Sunday services as worship. This is a mistake. The prayer and praise of God's people in Ezra 3 in song and the preaching of God's Word by Haggai and Zechariah in Ezra 5:1–2 was a help and an encouragement for God's people to worship God with their whole lives, and so it is for us today.

Ephesians 5:1–2 tells us, "Therefore be imitators of God, as beloved children. And walk in love, as Christ loved us and gave himself up for us, a fragrant offering and sacrifice to God." Loving, worshiping, and serving God and serving others in his name is the only fitting response to the supreme substitutionary sacrifice for sins made once for all on Calvary's tree by the Son of God who is the Savior of all who accept what he has done for them and begin to follow him as his disciples. His love saved us and surrounds us; it has forgiven us and has brought us into the family of God. We are called to become, with the Holy Spirit's help, more like the one who loves us so. He is worthy of our praise and worship.

O worship the Lord in the beauty of holiness,
Bow down before Him, His glory proclaim;
With gold of obedience, and incense of lowliness,
Kneel and adore Him: the Lord is His name.

—John Samuel Bewley Monsell[2]

4

Facing the Battle

EZRA 4—6:12

THOUGH I LOVE WATCHING a good film, I always find too many flashbacks confusing. The fine 2017 blockbuster film *Dunkirk* is an example. It took me a while to catch on that the film was telling three stories side by side—about a soldier, a sailor, and an airman—and the flashbacks to what happened that day were central to the film. In Ezra 4—6, the timeline moves around (especially in chapter 4) through different generations, but Ezra is making a point.

These chapters are most helpfully taught and preached together as they tell the story that God's people face opposition in each generation and that we are engaged in a spiritual battle continually. At first sight, the timeline in these chapters is somewhat confusing. It includes the reigns of four kings: Cyrus (539–530 B.C.), Darius (522–486 B.C.), Xerxes (Ahasuerus) (486–465 B.C.), and Artaxerxes I (464–423 B.C.). This covers more than a hundred years.

Ezra 4:1–5 deals with the rebuilding of the temple and opposition to that in the reigns of Cyrus and Darius. This part of the story continues from 4:24—6:22. However, the author, possibly Ezra himself, is looking back to this period from his own day and digresses from telling that part of the historical story by mentioning later opposition in the reigns of Xerxes and Artaxerxes, which interrupts the historical flow in the story as it is laid out for us. Why does he do that? Perhaps to make the important point that every believer needs to take in: each generation that is seeking to faithfully follow the Lord will find opposition from a world in rebellion against its Creator. The people of God have faced opposition at every stage in the unfolding of God's plan. We should expect no different. But this is also the story of opposition overcome and the undefeatable, advancing purposes of God.

Let us look at this opposition in more detail.

The World in the Church, Polite but Manipulative (4:1–3)

At first glance, the request from the people of the land to join the building project seems reasonable enough. Would not the returning exiles be glad of any help they could get in the big task that lay before them? Derek Kidner describes the situation well:

> The mention of the *king of Assyria who brought us here* provides a pointer to the story of 2 Kings 17:24ff. and another angle on the speakers and their religion. That story, in brief, tells of foreign communities who were forced to settle in the depopulated land of Israel after the fall of Samaria. To teach them "the law of the god of the land" an Israelite priest was eventually sent to them, but the outcome was only a mixture of religions: "they feared the Lord but served their own gods." The passage sums up bluntly what that really meant: "To this day they do according to the former manner. They do not fear the Lord." (2 Kings 17:34). . . .
>
> Such, then, is the uncompromising verdict of Scripture on the claim *we worship your God as you do*, when it is put forward as a multi-faith proposition. It was clearly the underlying reason for the Jews' reply. . . . [1]

It was help offered at too great a cost—it would lead to a disastrous multi-faith influence in the running of the temple! That compromise had led to tragedy in the past. The worship of God must be pure and for him alone; there are no other gods than the God of heaven and earth (5:11).

When I was vicar of a large, growing church in northeast London, we were delighted to have the opportunity to use the no-longer-used buildings of a health center next door to our church building. We were keen to do more social outreach projects in our parish and were willing to work with government social workers wherever we could. All this was enthusiastically welcomed by secular authorities until we said we would be sharing our faith, not in a forceful way but naturally as God gave us opportunity, with people we were seeking to help in these projects. We were told that they very much wanted the projects to go ahead as an expression of our Christianity, but that we must not share our faith. We sadly pulled out of this offered help financially and practically as far too costly an option. If we could not share the transforming love of Jesus with people, we would find other practical ways to facilitate that. Sometimes the world wants our cooperation and wants to be part of our Christian care but ultimately wants us to compromise our faith. This we must not do!

The Jews of Ezra's time were clearheaded and were right to serve God without compromise (4:3).

The World Seeking to Discourage (4:4–5)

If the appeal for involvement and influence didn't work, the next step was discouragement and bad-mouthing the motives and intentions of God's people. This has often been surprisingly successful in wearing down good intentions over the years. Delay tactics and objecting to planning permissions would be the modern equivalent. This delayed the building of the temple, which had been going well (5:8) for ten years and was only restarted again due to the God-sent preaching and encouragement of Haggai and Zechariah (4:24—5:2).

When I was serving as an area bishop in the County of East Sussex, England, the senior diocesan bishop was a fine and active man in his eighties. One day I received an extraordinary letter from some of the county aristocracy asking me to attend a meeting at which they would discuss ways to force the diocesan bishop to retire. It was couched as concern for the well-being of the church in the county. The signatories were largely people on the fringe of the church. I replied that I would go to no such meeting, as the bishop was a good and godly man, and I reminded them that Moses did his best work after he was eighty. Fringe church people might appear well-intentioned initially but can become fierce opponents of a Biblically obedient ministry.

The Jews at that time were foolish to let the opposition get to them and distract them from what God had called them to do. We will be equally foolish if the opposition of the world, the flesh, and the devil (however seemingly reasonable) browbeats us into a limp-wristed obedience, or worse, outright disobedience to what God want us to be and do.

The World Bringing Opposition to the Purposes of God

The Jews faced serious and powerful political opposition that appealed to the self-interest of the Persian kings. Let us look at the mounting opposition in its stages.

First, the pressure made the people afraid of what the opposition would do by distracting and frustrating their efforts to get on with the job (4:1–5). As a result, the work stopped for ten years (4:24).

Second, the governor and associates of the large Persian province "Beyond the River," of which they (Judah) were a smaller province (like a county within a state in U.S. terms), visited and threatened them, demanding to see the paperwork that had given them permission to build and also jotting down the names of the builders so they could be reported (5:3–5).

Third, the same governor then wrote to King Darius, reporting their visit and their request for evidence that the Jews had been given permission to build the temple, which was already progressing well. The Jews had been unable to produce evidence but faithfully told the story of how Cyrus had given them permission (5:13). The governor requested the paper trail and evidence for the issuing of the decree by Cyrus (5:17). Politely put, it even contained a recognition that the temple was dedicated to "the great God" (5:8). But there was no goodwill here; rather, there was powerful, planned opposition to the work in which the people of God were engaged (5:6–17).

Fourth, "an accusation" was written against the inhabitants of Judah and Jerusalem to King Xerxes (circa the time of Esther, some forty years later, 4:6).

Fifth, two letters of opposition were apparently written to Artaxerxes more than twenty years later. The first one was just mentioned (4:7a), and the second one elaborated on it and was written in Aramaic (4:8ff.). This was a cleverly written appeal to the king claiming to represent all the previous inhabitants of the whole province "Beyond the River." This spoke of the rebuilding of the city walls and the restoration of the city of Jerusalem and, looking back on the history of the powerful kings in Jerusalem, expressed concern for the security of the Persian king's control of that area; it also doubted his ability in the future to collect taxes ("the royal revenue will be impaired," 4:13). This complaint was supposedly expressed out of loyalty to the king. This had the desired effect on the king: "Therefore make a decree that these men be made to cease, and that this city be not rebuilt, until a decree is made by me. And take care not to be slack in this matter. Why should damage grow to the hurt of the king?" (4:21–22).

Whereas the earlier letters of appeal to stop the work on the temple were not successful, as we shall see, this one prevented the rebuilding of the walls until the time of Nehemiah (445 B.C.)

The opposition, then, was constant through the generations and was at times quite effective. God's people needed to *realize* that there would be opposition and not be surprised or thrown off by that, and also learn to *resist* that opposition in the power of the Lord.

How God Helped the People Resist and Finish the Building of the Temple

First, he sent prophetic preachers to challenge, encourage, and stand with the work force (5:1–2; 6:14–15). God's people always need the Word of God preached to them regularly, for that is the primary means of God's encouragement to his people as they hear again his promises to them, his steadfast love for them, and his promised help to enable them in the tasks he has called them to do. (Read Haggai 1—2 to see what he said to the people.)

Second, God encouraged them by his careful, providential watch over them. Despite the threatening visit of the provincial leaders, the builders, encouraged by strong leaders, kept going until they heard from the king himself as to whether they could continue. This was because the God who sees the need of his people comes down to help and deliver them (as he did at the time of the first deliverance from slavery in Egypt). "But the eye of their God was on the elders of the Jews, and they did not stop them until the report should reach Darius and then an answer be returned by letter concerning it" (5:5).

They were experiencing the presence of a watching, caring, enabling, and overruling God. This was seen too in the response of Darius (6:1–12), who found the records and who told the complainers (in a gesture that displayed God's providential prevention of interference) to "keep away. Let the work on this house of God alone" (6:6–7). He added threats to this (6:11–12). Furthermore, the enemies of God's people were instructed to provide "whatever is needed" (6:9) for the building and running of the temple, and that was to be funded out of the taxes they collected (thus those opponents had less for themselves—they should have kept quiet). Darius, with a similar outlook to that of Cyrus, hoped "that they may offer pleasing sacrifices to the God of heaven and pray for the life of the king and his sons" (6:10). All this came about because of the caring eye of God on his people, sovereignly helping them get the task done.

Third, they were challenged by God to persevere as his redeemed, restored, and faithful servants, and they discovered that God was helping them do just that (6:14)!

New Testament Perspective

While I do not find myself often quoting the late John Wimber, one of his analogies has stuck with me, and I have found it helpful indeed. He noted that when people become Christians they sometimes think that when they go down to the harbor to board the vessel of the King of kings, they will find a luxury liner; instead, they find a battered battleship. This side of Heaven we are called to battle the world, the flesh, and the devil. As Joni Eareckson Tada says so graphically, "It is only in Heaven that Kleenex will go out of business!" It is not until then that God "will wipe away every tear from their eyes, and death shall be no more, neither shall there be mourning, nor crying, nor pain anymore, for the former things have passed away" (Revelation 21:4). What a glorious prospect!

Going back to the battleship analogy, people tell me that on cruises on a luxury liner you may hear the following kind of conversation on the sun deck:

"That was a nice meal, but not as good as last night's. I prefer the chef in the Italian section!" On a battleship the conversations are quite different. Every sailor knows he must play his part in war; every role is crucial. If a gun is not prepared properly, the enemy might sink them first! The crew has a camaraderie unique to being in battle together as they wait for their captain's orders. It is literally all hands on deck.

Too often church people can have luxury-liner conversations. "I didn't like the music this week" or "I know the pastor is a good preacher, but his sermon last week was far better!" If we understand that we have a battle to fight and a mission in which to engage—reaching out to a lost world with the gospel of life and peace—our conversations would be very different. We are not spectators but participants in the Body of Christ, the Church.

What Ezra tells us so clearly about constant opposition is repeated in the New Testament to Christians. The supreme passage on this is Ephesians 6:10–20. As believers we have a battle to fight in the power of the Spirit. I have heard many sermons on "the whole armor of God" presented in that passage and the necessity of putting the various pieces on, spiritually speaking, and that is very important indeed. But I have heard much less emphasis on the verbs in this passage, which are equally important:

- *"Be strong* in the Lord and in the strength of his might"* (Ephesians 6:10).
- "*. . . Stand . . . withstand . . . stand firm . . . Stand* therefore" (Ephesians 6:11, 13–14).
- "*. . . Keep alert* with all perseverance" (Ephesians 6:18).
- *"Take up* the shield of faith" (Ephesians 6:16) in all circumstances; that is, trust the Lord.
- *Pray* "at all times in the Spirit . . . making supplication for all the saints" (v. 18). The weapons of our warfare are prayer and "the sword of the Spirit, which is the word of God" (v. 17). This side of Heaven we have a battle to face, and it is "not . . . against flesh and blood" but "against the spiritual forces of evil in the heavenly places" (v. 12).

Let us not expect an easy ride but face the battle, and in it prove again and again the steadfast love of the Lord who is with us and the power of his might in our struggles. Prayer and trust in his Word is the path of help, strength, and victory. He has promised his strength and help.

God made this plain to his people of old too.

"This is the word of the LORD to Zerubbabel: Not by might, nor by power, but by my Spirit, says the LORD of hosts. Who are you, O great mountain? Before Zerubbabel you shall become a plain. And he shall bring forward the top stone amid shouts of 'Grace, grace to it!'" Then the word of the LORD came to me saying, "The hands of Zerubbabel have laid the foundation of this house; his hands shall also complete it. Then you will know that the LORD of hosts has sent me to you. For whoever has despised the day of small things shall rejoice, and see the plumb line in the hand of Zerubbabel." (Zechariah 4:6–10)

Be strong, O Zerubbabel, declares the LORD. Be strong, O Joshua, son of Jehozadak, the high priest. Be strong, all you people of the land, declares the LORD. Work, for I am with you, declares the LORD of hosts, according to the covenant that I made with you when you came out of Egypt. My Spirit remains in your midst. Fear not. (Haggai 2:4–5)

These truths are also well expressed in a contemporary Christian song:

> O church, arise and put your armor on;
> Hear the call of Christ our captain;
> For now the weak can say that they are strong
> In the strength that God has given.
> With shield of faith and belt of truth
> We'll stand against the devil's lies;
> An army bold whose battle cry is "Love!"
> Reaching out to those in darkness.
>
> Our call to war, to love the captive soul,
> But to rage against the captor;
> And with the sword that makes the wounded whole
> We will fight with faith and valor.
> When faced with trials on ev'ry side,
> We know the outcome is secure,
> And Christ will have the prize for which He died—
> An inheritance of nations.

—Keith Getty and Stuart Townend*

5

The Temple Finished and Dedicated

EZRA 6:13–22

THIS PASSAGE IS A LOVELY summary of what the book has been teaching so far. The temple was completed, against all odds, in 516 B.C. This was because God had helped and enabled them. How did he do this?

- By turning the heart of the king of Assyria, so that he aided them in the work (6:22).
- By sending prophets who taught them God's Word, challenging and encouraging them (6:14).
- By enabling them, by his presence with them, to be obedient and to get on with the job he had called them to do (6:14).

Their response was to celebrate and to dedicate the temple (6:16).

- They celebrated with a God-given joy (6:16, 22).
- They kept the Passover for all "the returned exiles," knowing that their continuing status and blessing as God's people depended on the substitutionary sacrifice that God had provided for the forgiveness of their sins (6:19–20).
- They showed "a passive concern of postexilic Judaism . . . that all things be done in precise conformity with what was written in the Mosaic Law."[1]
- Along with all who would join them from neighboring nations, they dedicated themselves afresh to God, understanding that he had called them to be holy and set apart from other people for his worship and service. So they kept the Feast of Unleavened Bread with joy (6:22).

- They realized that their life as God's people and the joy they experienced was a direct result of God's grace in redeeming and restoring them. They owed it all to him!

When God is at work in revival and renewal, a similar joyful response will always be found! May he make those of us who by God's grace are his covenant people today equally responsive and joyful!

6

"Lord, Please Do It Again"

EZRA 7

THE BOOK OF EZRA does not tell us about the spiritual state of the Jews between the completion of the temple in 516 B.C. and the coming of Ezra to Jerusalem in 458 B.C., though it is likely that Zechariah 9—14 and the book of Malachi speak into that situation. Also, the book of Esther tells us how the Jews were doing in Persia. However, it is clear that all was not well and that the blessing of the earlier years needed to be repeated and continued. Revival needs to be prayed for and longed for in each generation.

Turn the clock forward eighty years from the decree of Cyrus to 458 B.C., some fifty-eight years after the temple was built. Ezra himself now appears on the scene (Ezra 7, 8). There was still a great need in Jerusalem. An attempt to build the walls had failed (4:12, 21, 23), and therefore the city remained insecure. The temple needed refurbishment and probably repairs (7:27).

Because not as many people had returned after the exile as had originally been hoped for, more needed to be done, and a new generation needed to be challenged to return to populate the land and complete the task of restoration. So God raised up Ezra as that much-needed leader. He was highly thought of by the Persian king (note the warmth toward him in the king's decree in chapter 7). Ezra had clearly commended himself by the dedication and consistency of a life lived well, and he was now given the opportunity to help his people. Following his request to the king, he seemed to be a sort of Secretary of State for Jewish Affairs.[1] He was also well qualified from a Jewish point of view as a priest who had become an important scribe and was from the family of the Aaronic-Zadokite high priestly line (7:1–5).

The Hand of the Sovereign Lord at Work Again

This is an amazing story, and the king's generosity is seen in his decree, which was drafted for him by Ezra himself. Those who wanted to return with Ezra could do so. The king decreed five things:

1. He commissioned Ezra and those who would go with him to investigate the spiritual state of things in Jerusalem, measured by the peoples' obedience to "the Law of your God, which is in your hand" (the Pentateuch at least) (7:14).
2. Money was provided to buy animals for sacrifice and any necessary supplementary vessels for those that had previously been returned (7:15–20).
3. The treasurers of the province "Beyond the River" were to give financial and practical support (7:21–23).
4. No temple official, priest, or servant was to be taxed (7:24).
5. Ezra was authorized to set up a judicial system to administer the Law of God, "the wisdom of your God that is in your hand" (7:25), and to teach it to those who were ignorant about it (7:25–26).

In short, Ezra had the twofold task of:

• Assessing the spiritual state of the church in Jerusalem and Judea.
• Carrying the gifts of gold and silver from the king to the temple in Jerusalem.

The king's motivation was fear that he would offend "the God of heaven" (7:23), which would endanger himself and his sons. It seems that the king wanted to keep peace with any deity among his people who might cause him trouble, so he adopted a supportive role toward all gods, maybe especially the God of the Jews. He had already had trouble in Egypt, having dispatched an army there that same year, so he did not want additional trouble in Jerusalem.

Artaxerxes was clearly impressed with Ezra's learning and lifestyle (7:6, 10b) and granted his requests to enable him and others to go to Jerusalem as emissaries of the king. Ezra had the influence that he did because he was admired. This is a good reminder to us all to live in a way that commends our faith to the unbelievers among whom we mix. People are more likely to accede to our requests if they see the reality of a godly life lived out faithfully.

Ezra had set his heart to "study the Law of the Lord," and not only that but to "do it," to live it out (7:10). This is authentic, godly living that sees the connection between doctrine and practice. Theology is meant to lead to doxology (praise to God) and to sound and healthy living (holiness of life). But Ezra also knew that his success with the king was due to God's power and influence making the journey to Jerusalem possible (7:6, 9, 27–28), enabling him against all human odds to do good for the Lord's people.

Ezra learned the Word of God, lived it out faithfully and attractively, and loved to teach it to the people. This is a good description of a faithful priest and can be applied to pastors and elders, otherwise called overseers in New Testament times (Titus 1:5, 7). What an impact such a life can make!

Ezra is described as a scribe—that is, one learned in the Law of God and given to its translation and teaching. The role of the scribes, modeled on Ezra's example, became more important in the postexilic Second Temple period and can be seen in the respect they held in New Testament times among the people, even when many were no longer following the godly example of Ezra.

There is a lovely section at the end of chapter 7 where we read that Ezra, having a heart full of praise and adoration, gave all the credit to God, "who put such a thing as this in the heart of the king, to beautify the house of the LORD that is in Jerusalem" (7:27). Ezra knew that he was seeing and experiencing the wonderful, covenant, "steadfast love" of God to him and at work among the king and his advisers for the good and blessing of his people (7:28). That is what gave him courage and enabled him to set about gathering leaders to journey with him. Whenever we lack the incentive or courage to get on with God's work and his call upon our lives, the recognition of his presence, help, strength, and encouragement—all wrapped up in his promises—motivates us to be up and at it.

The Heart of a Leader and the Kind of People God Uses

When God brings about a time of revival among his people, there is always a new love for the Word of God, which includes both a delight in its promises and a new determination to obey its commands. So it was in the time of Ezra. It is not at all surprising that it was this kind of leader, with these kinds of hallmarks, that God raised up for the job. We have considered how the priorities of Ezra's life shone and impressed the king and how God used his godly life to gain an opportunity to lead the second batch of exiles home to Jerusalem. There he would be used by God to bring about a new time of refreshing and revival, as we shall see. Let me simply summarize the notable things about Ezra as an example of a leader used by God:

- He studied God's Word. He took the time to study it and fully consider its serious implications (7:10).
- He sought more than intellectual knowledge, praying earnestly for help to live it out himself before he taught others (7:10b).

- He loved to teach God's Word to others and saw that as a key and crucial part of his role. He knew that knowledge of God and his Word brought progress and joy to God's people. God gave him a rich opportunity to further that ministry (7:25).
- His life and ministry were conducted in thankfulness to God, who alone enabled him to be used and to succeed in his tasks (7:9, 28).

What a fantastic example Ezra leaves us with, not only for all future priests who are scribes, but also for those who are called to minister to God's people under the terms of the new covenant, who are called to be ministers of his Word. Malachi, writing perhaps some thirty years later, had to remind the priests of a good example and warn them how far from that their practice had fallen (Malachi 2:5–9).

Here again in this chapter we see the God who reigns, working for the restoration and blessing of his people and providentially ruling and overruling for them, so that yet another exodus could take place. God was reviving his people again!

New Testament Perspectives

We see the value of the teaching of God's Word in many passages in the New Testament. For example, "All Scripture is breathed out by God and profitable for teaching, for reproof, for correction, and for training in righteousness, that the man of God may be complete, equipped for every good work" (2 Timothy 3:16–17). We also read:

> I charge you in the presence of God and of Christ Jesus, who is judge of the living and the dead, and by his appearing and his kingdom: preach the word; be ready in season and out of season; reprove, rebuke, and exhort, with complete patience and teaching. For the time is coming when people will not endure sound teaching, but having itching ears they will accumulate for themselves teachers to suit their own passions, and will turn away from listening to the truth and wander off into myths. As for you, always be sober-minded, endure suffering, do the work of an evangelist, fulfill your ministry. (2 Timothy 4:1–5).

See also Paul's example of living and teaching to the Ephesian church elders, in Acts 20:17–38. For example, "I did not shrink from declaring to you the whole counsel of God. Pay careful attention to yourselves and to all the flock, in which the Holy Spirit has made you overseers, to care for the church of God, which he obtained with his own blood" (Acts 20:27–28). We see here that Paul's concern was twofold:

1. That the elders teach the gospel of repentance and faith in the Lord Jesus Christ by teaching "the whole counsel of God" (Acts 20:27; see also vv. 21, 24). It is important for our church congregations to be taught all of God's Word, not just the easy bits or our favorite bits!
2. That teaching and preaching must be backed up, as it was in Ezra's case, by a godly life that pays "careful attention to [yourself] and to all the flock," remembering you have the great privilege "to care for the church of God" (Acts 20:28).

That kind of Bible teaching ministry will always be key in God's work of restoring and reviving his church. As we use the following hymn as a prayer, let us pray that God raises up more ministers with the heart and determination of both Ezra and Paul.

Restore, O Lord,
The honour of Your name,
In works of sovereign power
Come shake the earth again;
That all may see
And come with reverent fear
To the living God,
Whose kingdom shall outlast the years.

Restore, O Lord,
In all the earth Your fame,
And in our time revive
The church that bears Your name.
And in Your anger,
Lord, remember mercy,
O living God,
Whose mercy shall outlast the years.

Bend us, O Lord,
Where we are hard and cold,
In Your refiner's fire
Come purify the gold.
Though suffering comes
And evil crouches near,
Still our living God
Is reigning, He is reigning here.

—*Graham Kendrick and Chris Rolinson**

7

Believers Face Challenges

EZRA 8

IT IS ONE THING TO KNOW that God has called you to a mission in Jerusalem, but you have to get there first. That journey took Ezra four months and was both dangerous and difficult. What needed to be done to make this journey successful?

Establishing Identity

Knowing who was with you and establishing your clear identity was again very important (as it had been in the first return; see Ezra 2). This time the numbers were much smaller: just over 1,400 men, plus the thirty-eight Levites eventually gathered, plus 200 temple servants—1,674 in total (8:1–21). Adding women and children made the number probably about 5,000.

Wise Leadership in Action

Ezra noticed several situations that required wise, decisive leadership. In response to Ezra's faith, God provided him with the wisdom he needed for the benefit of the people and for God's glory (8:15–34).

Things Needed to Get Going in the Right Way

Review of the People and the Requirements for the Journey

Ezra gathered and reviewed an assembly of all who would journey with him (8:15). He noticed the lack of Levites. We can only speculate about the reason for this. Maybe they felt that the key Levitical posts would already have been taken in Jerusalem and that they would have more use (or maybe status) by staying with the exiles in Babylonia. Whatever the reason, Ezra collected a small number (8:18–19), along with more temple servants (8:20). He espe-cially recruited the help of Joiarib and Elnathan, who were "men of insight," that is, skilled teachers and expounders/interpreters of the Law of Moses whose ministry complemented that of the Levites named in 8:16. He needed their help to fulfill the command of the king and to achieve his own desire to teach the Word of God to those who did not know it (7:25). He gathered all the help he could for the journey, knowing who exactly was with him.

Fasting and Prayer

Ezra called everyone to fast and pray, realizing their utter dependence on God's grace and mercy (fasting as a practice became a higher priority after the exile) (8:21). They needed God's presence and help if they were to return home safely and fulfill their tasks. The people were called to repentance and prayer as essen-tial at the very beginning of their adventure of faith, which the journey certainly was. Humility, rather than self-confident arrogance, is always best expressed in prayerfulness, which expresses better than anything else that we cannot do God's will in our own strength; we need his help to live out his will for our lives.

Ezra had spoken to the king with confidence about God's protection of and goodwill toward his people, and now he was shamed into actually believ-ing it and putting his faith into practice (8:22). Nehemiah later availed himself of a military escort (Nehemiah 2:9), but here God asked his people to depend on him alone for protection along the way. The journey would have been es-pecially hazardous because of bandits due to the wealth of silver, gold, and temple vessels they were carrying. But God listened to their heartfelt prayers and protected them and their families along the whole way (8:21–23). What a lesson they learned from that experience!

Shared Responsibility

As a good leader, Ezra knew the importance of delegation, and he entrusted the care of all the valuables to the priests, who would have to give a careful account for everything to the temple officials when they arrived. They were set apart for the Lord's service, and it was appropriate that they should take care of all those gifts set apart to aid temple worship in Jerusalem (8:28–30).

Good Stewardship

Many church efforts have faltered because of poor stewardship. Not so here. Ezra made sure that everything was weighed and records kept (8:34). Every-thing needed to be seen to be above board.

The initial delay in departure (8:15, 31) was necessary to get things sorted out, but in due course they arrived, due to God's protection and care (8:31–32). On the fourth day, after three days of recovery time, they handed over their precious cargo (8:33–34).

After their arrival (8:35–36), they did three things:

- They offered burnt offerings to the Lord. Grateful for safe travel and knowing their status as God's people was based on the forgiveness provided by God in his grace and mercy, they rightly put the Lord first and dedicated themselves afresh to him.
- They remembered what they had been asked to do by the king, and they set about doing it. They remembered that though they were free, they were also servants, ultimately of God.
- They supported local believers whom they had come to join and help.

Much can be learned from Ezra's wise leadership of God's people here that can be applied to the wisdom needed to lead a congregation of God's people today as followers of Christ. We especially need to remember, as John Bunyan so brilliantly pictured in *The Pilgrim's Progress*, that if we are true Christians, we are on a journey to Heaven, a journey that will test our faith and on which we will need to depend on God for his protection, care, and help. He promised to provide all that and to lead us home, and he surely will, just as he did for those people of old on their journey to the promised land.

New Testament Perspectives

We perhaps see this most clearly fulfilled toward the end of the New Testament:

> And I saw the holy city, new Jerusalem, coming down out of heaven from God, prepared as a bride adorned for her husband. And I heard a loud voice from the throne saying, "Behold, the dwelling place of God is with man. He will dwell with them, and they will be his people, and God himself will be with them as their God. He will wipe away every tear from their eyes, and death shall be no more, neither shall there be mourning, nor crying, nor pain anymore, for the former things have passed away." (Revelation 21:2–4)

Christian believers, be encouraged—we have a future and a hope! A traditional African hymn expresses this powerfully:

> We are marching in the light of God,
> We are marching in the light of God.
> We are marching, marching,

We are marching, marching,
We are marching in the light of God.

We are living in the love of God,
We are living in the love of God.
We are living, living,
We are living, living,
We are living in the love of God.

We are moving in the power of God,
We are moving in the power of God.
We are moving, moving,
We are moving, moving,
We are moving in the power of God.

—*Anders Nyberg and Andrew Maries*[1]

8

The Danger of Dilution

EZRA 9

THE NEXT TWO CHAPTERS of Ezra describe a serious pastoral problem that threatened the identity and integrity of the people of God in that day. The problem is stated succinctly in 9:1–2:

> The people of Israel and the priests and the Levites have not separated them-selves from the peoples of the lands with their abominations. . . . For they have taken some of their daughters to be wives for themselves and for their sons, so that the holy race [or offspring; see ESV footnote] has mixed itself with the peoples of the lands. And in this faithlessness the hand of the of-ficials and chief men has been foremost.

In other words, there was no concern for holiness in family life. They had forgotten that at home too they were meant to be God's holy people dedicated to him and obedient to his commands. Because of the danger of spiritual dilu-tion and the influence of pagan wives on their children and family life, God had commanded:

> When the LORD your God brings you into the land that you are entering to take possession of it, and clears away many nations before you, the Hittites, the Girgashites, the Amorites, the Canaanites, the Perizzites, the Hivites, and the Jebusites, seven nations more numerous and mightier than you, and when the LORD your God gives them over to you, and you defeat them, then you must devote them to complete destruction. You shall make no covenant with them and show no mercy to them. You shall not intermarry with them, giving your daughters to their sons or taking their daughters for your sons, *for they would turn away your sons from following me, to serve other gods.* Then the anger of the LORD would be kindled against you, and

he would destroy you quickly. But thus shall you deal with them: you shall break down their altars and dash in pieces their pillars and chop down their Asherim and burn their carved images with fire.

For you are a people holy to the LORD your God. The LORD your God has chosen you to be a people for his treasured possession, out of all the peoples who are on the face of the earth. (Deuteronomy 7:1–6)

The issue then is not an ethnic one but a religious one![1] God must have first place in the hearts and lives of his people, and that devotion must not be undermined by a religious syncretism (worship of God and other gods as well) or by an abandonment of God for other gods. This would destroy the identity and holiness of God's people and would undermine proper godliness in family life. Because of sin, believers and their children can easily be seduced into a less-than-wholehearted devotion to the Lord, the only true God. So the issue is fundamental to the health and well-being of the church of the day.

As if this was not bad enough, the Jewish spiritual leaders—the priests and Levites—as well as the secular leaders were in the vanguard of this disobedient folly (9:1–2). The leaders therefore were faithless and compromising and were especially to blame. As F. C. Holmberg comments, "A covenant community that allows its leaders to adopt a life-style that threatens the central covenant torah traditions is sacrificing its future."[2]

Ezra described this behavior by Israel's leaders and the people as "faithlessness" several times (9:2, 4; 10:6, 10) and as a forsaking of God's commandments (9:10); it was therefore a disregarding of God's covenant of grace with them (Deuteronomy 7:9–11). They were forgetting the prime commandment of the God whose grace and mercy had redeemed and forgiven them and whose steadfast love was present with them and was the reason for their current blessing (Ezra 9:8–9). He had earlier told them, "You shall be holy to me, for I the LORD am holy and have separated you from the peoples, that you should be mine" (Leviticus 20:26).

What was involved in the "abominations" (9:14) that the pagan worship of the surrounding peoples had included are graphically described in Psalm 106:34–39:

They did not destroy the peoples,
   as the LORD commanded them,
but they mixed with the nations
   and learned to do as they did.
They served their idols,
   which became a snare to them.
They sacrificed their sons

and their daughters to the demons;
they poured out innocent blood,
     the blood of their sons and daughters,
whom they sacrificed to the idols of Canaan,
     and the land was polluted with blood.
Thus they became unclean by their acts,
     and played the whore in their deeds.

This fundamental requirement remains for believing Christians today. "As obedient children, do not be conformed to the passions of your former ignorance, but as he who called you is holy, you also be holy in all your conduct, since it is written 'You shall be holy, for I am holy'" (1 Peter 1:14–16).

Therefore Christians are told, because of the danger of undermining this holiness and diluting it, not to marry unbelievers (2 Corinthians 6:14–18). I have seen too many mixed marriages and the effects pastorally to ever doubt the wisdom of this instruction. The New Testament advice as to how to act toward an unbelieving partner is different from that followed in Ezra's particular historical situation (see 1 Corinthians 7:12–16: stay in the relationship if you can, and live as an example lovingly and prayerfully). Nevertheless, unmarried persons should marry whom they wish but "only in the Lord" (1 Corinthians 7:39). The holiness of the church matters today too, and its integrity and identity must not be undermined at home by a partnership with differing religious commitments. We are to be holy to the Lord, who has loved us and saved us by the death of his Son. The God who invented family life wants the best for it and wants to bless it; any disobedience here undermines our commitment to him and our acknowledgment that he knows what is best for us in the long run.

We are not told how much time is indicated by "after these things had been done" (9:1). But if we assume it was the same year, it is now four months later, December. No doubt Ezra had been fulfilling the king's commission (7:25) and his divine calling (7:10) by teaching the Law of God to as many as possible. There may have been assemblies like the one later described in Nehemiah 8. Whatever his method, his teaching was having an effect, and some were waking up to the fact that Israel was not behaving as a holy nation should. So they reported the situation to Ezra, knowing that these things were of great importance. Of the nations mentioned in 9:1, the first four no longer existed as ethnic groups, but the last three were identifiable pagan nations around Judah. They were describing their present problem in term of their old enemies. They were still surrounded by religious practices that were syncretistic, which put pressure on them to compromise in their worship of the one true God, Yahweh.

Ezra's reaction is worth careful attention:

He was appalled by the extent and seriousness of the problem and expressed his grief and utter dismay by tearing his garments and pulling out some of his hair. This was a sign of deep mourning and consternation. He let his response to the news be clearly seen, which had an effect on those of like concern. They gathered around him, sitting in sad silence until the evening sacrifice (9:3–4). Here was the reaction of a godly leader who "trembled at the words of the God of Israel" (9:4, cf. Isaiah 66:2) as he considered the state of the church and nation.

This concern drove him to cast himself on the Lord in prayer in very personal terms (note "my God" twice in 9:6). From then onward he referred to "our God" (9:8–10, 13) as he identified with the sin of the community he belonged to and served (though himself innocent). This is an important lesson for Christian leaders: they must make sure they identify with, and not stand above, the congregation that they are part of and to which they seek to minister. His prayer had three sections:

- The recalling of Israel's history and the guilt that had accrued to them over the years due to their disobedience of God and his Word (9:6–7).
- The steadfast love of God that had not given up on them. Rather, in his mercy and grace, he had brought them into this situation of revival and restoration by bringing them home to build the temple (9:8–9).
- Astonishment that despite the lessons of the past they were repeating their failures all over again, having "forsaken your commandments" (9:10). From verse 11 onward, Ezra recalled a collection of scriptures that underlined the problem, essentially focusing on Deuteronomy 7:4 and its warning. He acknowledged that God had punished them as a people less than they deserved and asked the Lord with astonishment, "Shall we break your commandments again and intermarry with the peoples who practice these abominations? Would you not be angry with us until you consumed us, so that there should be no remnant, nor any escape? . . . Behold we are before you in our guilt, for none can stand before you because of this" (9:14–15b). L. Allen and T. Laniak add, "For the people to continue would show both ingratitude and disregard of the grim warning of history. . . . This was not a God to be provoked by further sinning!"[3]

There was a glimmer of hope in Ezra's prayer that will become clearer in the next chapter. He knew that God's justice requires that he punish sin (9:15), but he also knew that God is just when he righteously forgives the repentant sinner, having made provision for salvation and restoration. Ezra was saying,

"We don't deserve it, but please be merciful again!" God had kept a "remnant" (9:14b–15) and was working out his long-term plan of grace, which was only yet partially fulfilled. So there was hope.

According to Mervin Breneman, "Ezra knew how important this 'remnant' was for God's plan. Only a pure and separate 'remnant' would be useful to God in his plan of redemption, which was to provide the Scriptures and the Saviour for all the world. This helps explain Ezra's seemingly 'radical' policies."[4] But for now all they could do was cast themselves on the mercy of God as undeserving sinners.

Ezra showed great wisdom as a leader. He took the time to gather like-minded people around him and to let the community realize the seriousness of the problem. His teaching of God's Word was known and was having an effect, he showed his profound distress and concern about the "faithlessness" of the returned exiles in not living by that Word, he led in prayer and by example, and he waited on God to see what developed. "Ezra's reaction was typical of him. It was almost inaction, yet more potent than any flurry of activity, since it drew out of other people the initiatives that could best come from them."[5]

Any serious matter of pastoral practice that affects a community and requires repentance and possible disciplinary action cannot be handled by one person, but must be given time to let people see what is at stake. Decisive action is needed in such a situation, but it must have the backing of the church of the day behind it. As we shall see, it was not long before a suggestion by way of a possible solution was forthcoming (10:2ff.)!

New Testament Perspectives

A distinctively different way of life is the calling of every true believer. We are to "walk" with the Lord in a way that shows itself in our attitudes and lifestyle (see Ephesians 4:1, 17; 5:2, 8, 15). It is a tragedy when we look no different than the world. We have been saved "to be conformed to the image of his Son" (Romans 8:29), that is, to become more like the Lord Jesus who saved us. That will only happen when we refuse to be conformed to the values of this world, and instead with thankfulness in our hearts for all God's goodness and mercy to us, seek with the Holy Spirit's help to let the teaching and values of God's Word shape us and fashion us anew (Romans 12:1–2).

9

Holiness Matters

EZRA 10

BEFORE CONSIDERING THE DRASTIC action taken in this chapter to solve the interfaith marriage problem, two striking things are worth noting.

The Nature of Ezra's Leadership

Above all he was concerned for faithfulness to God and obedience to his Word. He was prayerful and allowed the people to see what was on his heart, so they too could be convinced of what needed to be done without undue pressure from him. "Ezra's style of leadership repays study. As elsewhere (e.g., 9:1; Neh. 8:1), so here, he waited for the people to approach him. By teaching, patience and example, he was thus able to bring them without coercion to make for themselves the decisions he considered beneficial."[1]

The Effect of Godly Teaching and Example on a Believing Community

The new sensitivity to God and his commands and the importance of obedience to them in every area of their lives was the work of God in reviving and renewing his church. The people gathered in larger numbers, weeping because of their foolish disobedience that had strained the covenant obligations and endangered their identity as the people of God. They understood their sin and the seriousness of the situation they were now in, deserving God's judgment again. This kind of consciousness of sin is not drummed up by any human agency but is the work of God bringing illumination through the teaching of his Word. The faithfulness and integrity of Ezra's teaching and example was having an effect on the consciences of the people, who knew that weeping was not enough and that they had to take action to show repentance and correct their sinful behavior.

Most scholars think Malachi was a contemporary of Ezra and Nehemiah and that his ministry possibly predated that of Ezra. "If Ezra came to Jerusalem in 458 B.C., Malachi might belong to the previous decade. . . . The words of Malachi had already quickened the public conscience."[2] Perhaps his teaching also had an impact in changing hearts and lives and was being used by God in this awakening.

The people have come to a point of conviction reminiscent of the response to Peter's preaching on the Day of Pentecost: "What shall we do?" (Acts 2:37). Now this great assembly of men, women, and children knew in their hearts what had to be done, and Shecaniah expressed the consensus powerfully (10:2ff.). He expressed:

- Remorse, also felt deeply by the people (10:1–2).
- Remembrance of the covenant, recognizing that God is gracious and merciful and therefore there was hope (10:2b–3). They needed to renew their side of the covenant promises (10:5).
- Repentance. Action was desperately needed to redress the situation caused by their faithlessness (10:3).
- Response. When challenged by Ezra to confess their sin and show repentance, the people responded in agreement. Radical action had to be carried out in a carefully considered way and not rushed, so that justice was done (10:12–14).

Notice that Ezra's public and dramatic expression of concern and grief (10:1) was not just for show. It was backed up by a night of personal agonizing and prayer (10:6) plus decisive action as their leader in calling for a serious assembly (with penalties attached for nonattendance, 10:7–8) and an address that went straight to the heart of the problem (10:10–11).

We need to carefully consider the proposed drastic action:

Their identity and integrity as God's people was at stake. If not careful, they could become unidentifiable as the people who worshiped the true God alone. Their ability to be the people who would fulfill the promise to Abraham and deliver a Messiah for the whole world was in jeopardy.

They deserved God's judgment for their disobedience. Where would that leave them?

Those wives who wished to renounce false worship and be faithful only to God would presumably be allowed to remain (cf. 6:21), maintaining families that worshiped and followed only God. Though Ezra tells us nothing about the provision for persistent unbelieving wives and children (10:44), according to the conventions of the day they would have returned to their original families and homes.

According to Malachi, God hates divorce and was appalled that Jewish wives who married when young were being traded in for newer pagan models (Malachi 2:10–16). Notice that what God seeks by his commands is "godly offspring," that is, a united family that produces believers and worshipers of him (Malachi 2:15b). Maybe this is the background that Ezra was facing, which made the people's sin even more serious.

The list of names (10:18–44) shows two things:

- The rot was in every quarter of Jewish society and affected their leaders as well as everyone else.
- The problem was serious but not huge (it appears that around 110 families were affected). But the problem needed to be addressed individually and carefully by leaders who knew what was going on locally (10:14).

New Testament Perspectives

God remains concerned that believers marry believers so they can share what is of crucial spiritual importance together and know the joy of that, producing believing families as a result (1 Corinthians 7:39; 2 Corinthians 6:14). Believers and the church today are, generally speaking, greatly weakened by mixed marriages.

The particular drastic, family-splitting, heartbreaking action apparently required in Ezra's day because of the vulnerability of their national situation as "the holy race" (9:2) when the church coalesced with the nation is not needed or recommended under the terms of the new covenant, thankfully, since the church is transnational! As mentioned earlier, the advice of the New Testament as found in 1 Corinthians 7:12–16 and 1 Peter 3:1–6 encourages believers with unbelieving partners to do their best to keep the marriage together and to win their spouse to Christ by a life lived graciously that testifies and attracts others to him. But they are to let the unbeliever go if that spouse forsakes the marriage and the believer finds that he or she cannot save it.

———

A review of Ezra, the man and the book, is now helpful.

Ezra: The Profile of a Good Leader

He was first and foremost a man of God's Word, committed to its learning, living, and teaching (7:10).

He identified with the people God called him to serve (9:6–7).

He was thankful to God for his providential care of his people (7:27).

He was prayerful, knowing that nothing less than utter dependence on God expressed in prayer would see them through (8:21; 10:1).

He was faithful to God and to his Word (9:4). Those who tremble at God's Word, not just because of the weather (see 10:3, 9), are those who God esteems (cf. Isaiah 66:2).

He was brave (10:4–5). He called for repentance and obedience (10:11), but was encouraged to fulfill his leadership responsibility with the backing of the people in spite of any opposition (10:4, 15). "Popularity should never be the standard for judging the desirability of a policy, and if church leaders are undergirded by prayer, they will not be unwisely swayed by opposition."[3]

Lessons from the Book of Ezra

As we cast an eye back over Ezra and witness God's steadfast love to his people in rescuing, reviving, and restoring them, we are reminded of several important lessons.

We need Jesus, our shepherd-king, today to save us and bring us home to the new Jerusalem (Revelation 21:10ff.). It is because of his saving death for us that people of faith are redeemed since that first Easter, and before then too as they looked forward to the fulfillment of God's promises through what God would do at Calvary.

We ought to be thankful as we see the waywardness, fickleness, and sinful disobedience displayed in these people of old reflected in our own hearts and God's promises of a deeper and greater work of his Spirit under the terms of the new covenant (Jeremiah 31:31–34). He has given us a new heart to go his way and to help us in daily battles to obey his will.

We need the grace and truth that Jesus brings. Kings and leaders of old, however faithful, were flawed sinners. Jesus, the perfect God-man, is not only the unique revelation of God and the One who came to save us but also our model to live by (John 1:14, 18; 1 Peter 2:21–25).

Ezra, as Gordon McConville reminds us, is essentially prophetic writing. The revival stirrings of Ezra's day leave us wanting more. No Davidic king was on the throne again, they remained a vassal state, and the glory of the temple and the blessings on the nation were not yet all that God had promised. That longed-for period of blessing would only come in the complete fulfillment of God's promises and saving action in the Lord Jesus Christ, the King of kings and the Savior of the world. May the following be our heart's desire:

Holy Spirit, living breath of God,
Breathe new life into my willing soul.
Let the presence of the risen Lord,
Come renew my heart and make me whole.
Cause Your Word to come alive in me;
Give me faith for what I cannot see,
Give me passion for Your purity;
Holy Spirit, breathe new life in me.

*—Keith Getty and Stuart Townend**

The book of Ezra ends abruptly, but we need to remember Ezra—Nehemiah was originally one book. Ezra reappears again in happier circumstances in Nehemiah 8, characteristically teaching and preaching the Word of God at a time of a great revival.

* Extract taken from the song "Holy Spirit" by Keith Getty and Stuart Townend. Copyright © 2005 Thankyou Music (Adm. by CapitolCMGPublishing.com excl. UK & Europe, adm. at IntegrityRights.com).

NEHEMIAH

The Timeline of Nehemiah

516 B.C.
Temple Rebuilt

458 B.C.
**Ezra Arrives
in Jerusalem**

445 B.C.
**Nehemiah
Rebuilds Walls**

10

A Good Heart for God and His Work

NEHEMIAH 1

AN IMPORTANT QUESTION FOR all of us to ask is, How does the work of God get done? The book of Nehemiah answers that question. It lays out for us the foundational principles for any work of God.

It is important for us to realize that Nehemiah was, in the words of J. I. Packer, "a church builder."[1] Without the restoration of the walls of the city of Jerusalem, there could have been no normal or healthy city life. But the restoration of the walls was a means to an end—the restoration of the people of God in the city where God had promised to be especially present.

The covenant of grace recorded in the Old Testament often visualizes for us the spiritual principles spelled out in the New Testament. God is a God of consistent covenant (i.e., promise-keeping) grace in how he deals with his people, and the lessons they learned under the old covenant are beneficial to those of us blessed by the new covenant, won for us by the blood of our Savior, Jesus Christ.

Historical Background

A little bit of history to set the scene is necessary at this point. The one date that needs to be remembered more than any other is 586 B.C. Nebuchadnezzar, king of Babylon, destroyed Jerusalem, including the temple, and took the people into exile. God had warned his people, especially through Isaiah, that their persistent disobedience would bring this upon them. But God, in sheer grace, said that he would restore his people, and in 539 B.C. Cyrus, the Persian king, became God's instrument to bring this about. The people returned under Cyrus's decree (2 Chronicles 36:22–23; Ezra 1:1–11), but never in the hoped-for numbers. After a delay the temple was rebuilt, but it never recaptured the glory of Solomon's temple.

The year now is 446 B.C. (Nehemiah 1:1), twenty-two years after Ezra returned to Jerusalem. Previous attempts to rebuild the wall and restore the fortunes of Jerusalem had come to nothing (see Ezra 4:12ff.).

How did it come about that Nehemiah rebuilt the walls in record time (Nehemiah 6:15)? How did Nehemiah do what others had failed to do? How did the work of God get done in his generation?

The work of God gets done when there is a good heart for God and his work. It starts in a heart with a deep *concern* for the glory of God and the health of his church (or people).

Nehemiah met people from a camel train returning from Jerusalem, which included "one of my brothers" (1:2; whether a blood brother or a Judean brother we are not told, but most likely the former). He asked them about the state of things in Jerusalem because he was concerned, and their answer was even worse than he feared (1:3). The place was in ruins. In the words of David Jackman, "the work of God is paralysed and the people of God are demoralised."[2] Furthermore, says Raymond Brown, "broken walls meant frightening insecurity, negligible commercial development and serious economic deprivation, but the depressed people within the city were infinitely more important than its shattered walls."[3] Jerusalem was central to the purposes of God in Old Testament times. God had said he would be especially present in the temple as a reminder that he was in the midst of (that is, with) his covenant people.

Nehemiah was expressing a deep concern for the welfare of the people of God, the church of his day. The state of the church then caused him to weep, mourn, and above all, pray (1:4).

How concerned are you about the welfare of your church? We should be first concerned about the health and well-being of the congregation we are part of. In this day of a growing lack of commitment, when regular attendance at church can mean twice a month rather than twice a week, how committed are you to your church and how prayerful are you about its well-being? As a church warden (lay elder) once said to me, "If we prayed as often for our ministers as we are willing to criticize them, the church would be a much healthier place!"

Nehemiah was not only concerned about the well-being of his own congregation in Susa; he had a wider vision, and so should we. How concerned are you about the health of the church in your city or area? In your country? While we cannot meet the needs of Christians everywhere, we should have a concern to pray and support suffering believers in some particular part of God's world. Nehemiah wasn't parochial in vision or concern; he had wide horizons, and that concern drove him not to depression or a fatalistic attitude but to God in *prayer*.

Richard Lovelace, in his classic book *The Dynamics of Spiritual Life*,[4] describes how there was revival somewhere in the Western world each generation after the Reformation. When the church was in trouble or facing a big challenge, people were called upon to pray. Toward the end of the nineteenth century this experience of revival ceased. Lovelace suggests that the reason is because, at that time when the church was in trouble, a synod was called and meetings organized but the priority of serious prayer was neglected. There is nothing wrong with synods or meetings, but it is in prayer more than anywhere else that we express our dependence on God. We can't solve spiritual problems without radical dependence on him.

Nehemiah knew that, humanly speaking, the plight of Jerusalem and her people was hopeless. But he also knew that nothing was beyond God's power to change and help. So he prayed earnestly. It is easy for difficult or seemingly impossible situations to drive us in desperation to our friends, but Nehemiah's first recourse was to talk to God about it.

> What a friend we have in Jesus,
> All our sins and griefs to bear!
> What a privilege to carry
> Everything to God in prayer!
> O what peace we often forfeit,
> O what needless pain we bear,
> All because we do not carry
> Everything to God in prayer!
>
> —Joseph Scriven[5]

Nehemiah continued praying about the situation for several months (cf. 1:1 with 2:1). Look at the ingredients of his prayer.

The Prayer of Nehemiah

Confession

Nehemiah was the better part of a thousand miles away from Jerusalem. How could he be held in any way responsible for the plight in Jerusalem? But notice the use of "we," not "they," by Nehemiah (1:6–7). It is easy to blame others for problems, but Nehemiah knew that if God was judging the church of his day, he bore part of the blame. There had been disobedience in Judah, but he recognized the same willful disobedience in his own heart. Disobedience to the totality of God's commandments in the Pentateuch is summarized in verse 7. If God is judging the church in America or Britain (as I fear he is), then I am part of the problem, and along with all God's people, I too need to repent. Which one of us has been as zealous for the things of God as we should be or as faithful to his Word as he wants us to be? Repentance is the mark of a healthy Christian.

Covenant

Nehemiah addressed God in all his greatness and sovereign power (1:5). He is a God of covenant-keeping love. When in grace he enters into a relationship with his chosen people, he does not fail in his promises to them nor in his steadfast love toward them. He doesn't get tired of them nor drop his people. He doesn't give up on them. His love is sure and "steadfast" (1:5).

Further, in anthropomorphic language Nehemiah asked God to listen carefully to his prayer of desperation as well as asking God to open his eyes to the situation (1:6). Nehemiah could only pray to God like this because he knew God gives special attention to the cry of his people when they are in trouble (see for example Exodus 3:7–10; cf. Isaiah 37:17).

Conviction

Nehemiah had learned, or was learning, the secret of powerful and effective prayer, which is to pray the promises of God (1:8–9). Again, in very human terms he called on God to "remember" the particular promise he had made to his people (cf. Deuteronomy 4:25–31, especially v. 31). Nehemiah had deep confidence in a God who never breaks his word and is by nature a God of mercy and grace. He never forgot who God is and what he is like, and that gave Nehemiah's prayers wings. Nehemiah prayed daily like this for months! Do we give up too easily in our prayers? But notice two important things.

Firstly, by verse 11 he has gathered fellow believers to pray too. There was collective prayer, maybe even a prayer meeting in Susa.

Secondly, he was willing to be part of the answer to his own prayers. What could Nehemiah be expected to do so far away from the situation? He was at best an upwardly mobile slave and captive. But whatever God enabled him to do to help the situation, he was willing to do.

I heard a young minister preach recently about an imaginary church called St. Lukewarms, where they had rewritten a classic hymn to fit their lack of commitment. "Take my life and let it be, consecrated, Lord, to thee" had become "Take my wife and let me be"!

Nehemiah prayed for God to mercifully overrule in the situation. But he did not just have big ideas for others to do—"Take the minister or the deacons, but leave me be!" He was willing to seek an opportunity to do what he could. And he prayed for that opportunity to come each day (1:11).

Notice that in his prayer to God, he described the king differently than he would have addressed him in public. Before God and his power, the king was just "this man" (1:11), no different than any other.

Though Nehemiah had limitations as a captive, the end of verse 11 tells us that he was in a privileged position of trust as "cupbearer to the king." In those days, assassination of kings by poisoning their food or wine was not uncommon. The cupbearer was therefore a highly trusted member of the royal court whose loyalty to the king was not in doubt. We know that a cupbearer could become second only to the king (cf. Tobit 1:22 in the Apocrypha) and fulfill a sort of prime minister role. "That Nehemiah held this trusted post in the court of the Persian king Artaxerxes is an indication of the esteem and confidence that were afforded to certain Jews in foreign governmental service during this period."[6] But would the king let him do anything to help?

One thing was certain. The opulence and the privileges of Susa had not captured Nehemiah's heart. It was the honor of God and the importance of his name and work that had done that (1:11)!

This is an important point. Concern for the honor of God's name united Nehemiah and his friends. Their delight was in knowing and revering God's name (that is, who he is and all he had done, for his name reveals his character). They were hurt and sad when God's name was reviled and abused. The folly of idolatry was all too real to them in their situation. They had a zeal for the glory of God, which reflects in a little way the high priestly concern of the Son of God as he prayed just before his crucifixion (John 17:1ff.).

Are we hurt when God's name is used as a swear word or when people boast about their unbelief? I liked the large notice outside a good church I once saw, a provocative comment attributed to God to make people think: "I don't act as if you don't exist!"

Before we finish looking at chapter 1, an important question needs to be asked. Why did God delay in answering the prayers of his people over those months (November/December 446 B.C., 1:1; April/May 445 B.C., 2:1)? We know from the rest of the book that God intended to use Nehemiah to do his will. God was fashioning Nehemiah into a man of prayer. The delay was for his (and their) benefit. If it is true that "prayer is the most eloquent expression of our priorities"[7] and also the way in which we best express our dependence on God, then these months of prayer fashioned a habit in Nehemiah that is manifest all the way through the book and is the best explanation of Nehemiah's success. It was granted to him on his knees.

In review we have seen how Nehemiah:

- *Reviewed* the situation, with concern.
- *Responded* in prayer, confident in God's mercy and his faithfulness to his promises.
- *Requested* that God would help him to honor his name and reputation, act with God's help and approval, and that God would give him an opportunity to do what he could (1:11).

Now we will see what happened when the day of opportunity came.

11

Making the Most of the Opportunity!

NEHEMIAH 2:1–10

WE ARE NOW IN A POSITION to answer the question I posed at the beginning of the last chapter: How does the work of God get done? It gets done by a person with a concern for the glory of God and the well-being of his people, a *prayerful* heart that engages in persistent prayer with others, claiming God's promises, a *dedicated* and *involved* person who is ready and willing to be used by God. In every generation, these are the kind of people God raises up and uses to get his work done. Nehemiah was certainly like that.

In 2:1 we have come to April/May 445 B.C. After some five months of prayer, the day of opportunity arrived in a dramatic and dangerous way. Nehemiah looked sad, and that was noticed by the king, who interpreted this as possible ill will toward him. A top-ranking civil servant not being his usual joyful self in the king's presence could be the preliminary to a coup! This might have been met with a severe response from the king that put Nehemiah's life in danger; so it is not surprising that Nehemiah was "very much afraid" (2:2b). Nehemiah did not choose that day to appear sad in order to raise a question in the king's mind. This was like any other day when Nehemiah had prayed for an opportunity to make a difference and to be able to do something to help the well-being of God's people. He simply could not help showing his heart's concern. It was not sickness but sadness of heart that the king recognized, but not for the reason the king suspected.

Nehemiah now had the opportunity to explain himself and make his much thought and prayed about request to the king. He started well: "Let the king live forever!" He went on to explain in effect, "My sadness is not about you, O king, whom I hope lives and reigns for a long time. My sadness is because of the state of my ancestral city!" (see 2:3). This was a tactful and clever way of bringing the issue of the sad state of the church in Jerusalem before the king. Persian kings had a deep respect for their ancestors and their graves. So to mourn "the place of my fathers' graves" (2:3) was to present the need in an unthreatening way that would have maximum appeal to the king. The king, clearly moved, asked pointedly, "What are you requesting?" (2:4).

Notice that Nehemiah's response was to immediately back up his daily prayer with an arrow prayer as the opportunity arose (2:4b). Both kinds of prayer are necessary and needed in daily living.

He again talked about rebuilding the city of his fathers' graves (2:5), and when he got his foot in the door, he was not shy about asking for what was necessary to do the job. He asked for letters to the governors of the province on the way, for safe passage throughout (without which he would be vulnerable to attack and robbery), and also for a letter to the keeper of the king's forest, so that he could obtain the necessary timber to do the job in a tree-deprived and desolate Jerusalem (2:7–8). This daring was repaid with further generosity by the king, who sent a military escort along with Nehemiah (2:9).

The king understandably asked how long his trusted servant would be away from court (2:6). We are not told how long a leave of absence Nehemiah asked for, but we can safely assume that it was about two years, allowing for the journey time each way (four months plus) as well as the time to restore the walls and revitalize the city when he got there. He may only have asked for two years time away, but we learn later that his first term as governor was twelve years.

Notice the comment in parentheses in verse 6 "(the queen sitting beside him)." It was unusual for the queen to be present, and commentators legitimately speculate that it may well have been the king's birthday, when she would have been present with the king, and when the king would also be more likely to be feeling generous. She may also have put in a good word for Nehemiah; so her noted presence is significant. Considering how dangerous and manipulative courts could be in those days, perhaps the godly and trustworthy Nehemiah was something of a queen's favorite.

Be that as it may, it is important to remember that Nehemiah was asking the king to grant permission to do something the king had earlier refused to grant (Ezra 4:7, 12, 21, 23). But in God's timing and against human odds, the king now granted the request. Why? Nehemiah said, "The good hand of my God was upon me" (2:8). God was opening a door, answering prayer, and overruling a powerful earthly ruler to bring restoration and blessing to his people. He was raising up a leader who, though miles away, would be able to help and meet the need of his people in Jerusalem. Nehemiah was in no doubt whatsoever that without God's help and providential overruling, he could never have pulled it off with the king. God is, in Nehemiah's delightful phrase, "the God of heaven" (2:4b, 20; cf. 1:4–5). As J. Alec Motyer put it, "'God' points to one who possesses the fullness of the divine attributes, and 'heaven' to the fullness of his resources and of his executive power over earth."[1] He is the King of kings!

Notice that as soon as someone sets about to help the "welfare" of the church, there will be opposition (2:10). We will think more about Sanballat and Tobiah when we meet them later in the chapter (2:19).

Often we have longed for opportunities to speak up for our Lord, but if we are honest most of us have had far more opportunities than we had the courage to accept. Nehemiah's prayerful daring, waiting on God's time but brave when it came, is a wonderful and challenging example to us.

12

Sharing the Vision and
Starting the Work

NEHEMIAH 2:11–20

THE SCENE IN THIS DRAMATIC STORY changes now to Jerusalem. Nehemiah arrived, rested, and said nothing (2:11)! Imagine the speculation as the new governor arrived. What was going to happen? As always when there is a new government leader, the people wondered if there would be increased taxation. After three days he set out at night with a few trusted friends to examine the walls (2:12–13).

Raymond Brown said of Nehemiah, "He left the opulence of palatial surroundings for a dispirited community in a dilapidated city he had never seen."[1] He did this because the grace of God had captured his heart, as had the vision of what God wanted him to do about the situation (2:12).

Let us follow the steps of a wise leader as he sought to share the godly vision and mobilize the people of God into action.

Evaluation (2:13–16)

He set out by night with a few trusted friends to thoroughly evaluate the extent of the problem. This was essential groundwork. The debris was so bad that at one point, the mount he was riding could not get through (2:14). He kept his inspection private and said nothing to the spiritual or civic leaders about what he was doing until he had thoroughly evaluated the task at hand (2:16). But he was not a solo player, as he did have a few trusted friends around him to help analyze the situation.

We can learn a lot today from Nehemiah's example as a leader. A young couple I know in ministry moved to a new church situation that needed reviving. Among other things, they started a "mums and toddlers" work, a ministry that is often productive in making contacts for sharing the gospel. That work struggled, and eventually they closed it. A friend advised them to thoroughly evaluate the parish they were in, and they discovered that there were virtually no families with young children living in the area (the house prices were too high for first-time buyers). But there were lots of older children, and they started a work to reach them and were soon overflowing with family contacts. Proper evaluation of where God has called us to work for him is essential.

Vision (2:17)

Once the evaluation had been properly done, "then" Nehemiah shared the vision more widely (2:17). "You see the trouble we are in," he said (2:17a). Did they have a willingness to do anything about it? It is possible to live with and get used to the debris around us, both physically and spiritually. He was asking them to really see the situation and the challenge it presented.

Over the years I have noticed newly converted people often saying, when I inquired how they were doing, that being a Christian was great but that it seemed to be causing them more problems. "I seem to be more aware of sin and wrongdoing in my life than ever before" has been a relatively common complaint. They are initially surprised at my response: "That's good. The curtains in the room of your life have been pulled back, and Jesus, the Light of the world, is showing you what needs to be addressed and put right with his help."

As a good leader, Nehemiah identified with the people he was seeking to lead (he said "we" twice and "us" once in verse 17). We have seen this already in Ezra, and it is even more noticeable in Nehemiah. If God is judging the church we are part of, then we need to keep this principle in mind. Nehemiah had already acknowledged this in his daily prayer in Susa (1:6). Nehemiah did not put himself on a pedestal above his people but was one with them and was involved with them in the God-given task.

He also understood two key points about his calling.

- *The vision was God-given (2:12).* That had become crystal clear when the prayed-for opening was amazingly fruitful, when against all human odds the king had granted his requests. Nehemiah knew this would never have happened unless "the good hand of my God was upon me" in providential care and help (2:8).

- *The vision was people-driven (2:17b).* He needed to mobilize the whole people of God if the work was to get done. They were in a situation of shame and disgrace, and he appealed to them to do something about it.

Today we face an unfinished task (the great commission of our risen Savior and Lord to make disciples of all nations and so build his church). This task is not just for a few—all Christians are called to share the gospel far and wide.

Testimony (2:18)

Nehemiah testified to the fact of God's grace and providential involvement in the whole situation so far and how he had been enabled by God to come to Jerusalem to encourage them to rebuild the walls. Testimony to what God has done and is doing in our lives is powerful and compelling. I remember saying to a church where I was senior minister, "Every Sunday I should be able to walk among you with a microphone and ask each one of you what verse you have been blessed with this week or in what way God has been at work in your lives." They were initially somewhat scared by the prospect, but they got the message. If we are all walking with God, we will have testimonies to share.

Nehemiah testified about how God had brought about this opportunity and clearly wanted them to respond and set about doing the job. They caught the vision, were greatly encouraged by his testimony, and became motivated to start the strenuous task for the glory of God and, as a result, for their own blessing too (2:18b). The king and the King of kings (more importantly) wanted the walls rebuilt.

Do we share God's providential care for us as much as we should? It is easy to focus on the problems and the rubble rather than on what God wants us to do and will enable us to do for him.

Confidence (2:18, 20)

Nehemiah's confidence in God was infectious, and his confidence in God's people to respond was encouraging (2:18, 20). Nehemiah's confidence in God was informed by Scripture and God's promises therein, and also in his own experience of observing how God blesses those who seek to obey him according to his promises. Nehemiah was a confidence builder among God's people as he lifted their eyes beyond the rubble to the purposes of a gracious God for the well-being of his people. Are you a confidence-building Christian or do you quickly run to or dwell on the negative? However big problems may be, God is bigger!

It is heartening to observe how if we take a step of faith to fulfill God's purposes in the world, we find that God is already there ahead of us. When I was leading a church in northeast London, we needed an extra building to do a drop-in work with teenagers from the local school. The local government was selling off a suitable building that happened to be just across the road from the church. They wanted a huge amount for it, as they were cash-strapped. After much prayer we said we would pay for a full-time youth worker at the center and organize the events in the building for the community if they would give it to us on a lease for one pound a year. We got the requested lease for twenty years and also the part of the parking lot we requested even though they were planning to build on that. God had seen to it in his providence that, years earlier, drains had been laid under half of the parking lot so that it could not be built on, and we got what we needed, by his grace. A great work has been done at the center ever since then. We took one little step of faith into the community to reach a lost generation with the gospel, and God did amazing things to open doors. That dramatically encouraged and mobilized the church. (A fuller version of this event can be found in the part of this commentary on Esther, see page 171.)

Opposition Grows (2:19)

Formidable opposition mounted from outside the church (Geshem), but also from the fringes of the church (the name Tobiah means "Yahweh is good"). Here is the helpful description of the opposition by J. I. Packer:

> What are we to make of these angry men who became Satan's tools in opposing Jerusalem's restoration? . . . Sanballat's name is Babylonian. . . . Extrabiblical sources tell us that he was the elderly governor of Samaria in 407 B.C., thirty-eight years after Nehemiah came to Jerusalem and built the wall, and that his two sons bore Jewish names that celebrated Yahweh. The natural guess is that Sanballat was a non-Jew, though perhaps married to a Jewish woman, that he had already become governor of Samaria before Nehemiah arrived, that he had no religious interest or motivation of any kind, and that he was very anxious to carve out a career by showing himself a loyal servant of the Persian regime.
>
> He was, then, a thoroughly worldly man who opposed Nehemiah in order to keep his nose clean with his Persian masters and also, no doubt, to avoid the destabilizing emergence of a new power base less than forty miles from his own headquarters. . . .
>
> In this back-breaking construction job that Nehemiah had taken on, his goal must by elimination be profit or power or both. Worldlings today accuse Christians of the same self-serving purposes; there is nothing new under the

sun. The honor and praise of God as a motive for action clearly meant nothing to Sanballat, and in this he is typical of fallen mankind generally.

Tobiah ("Yahweh is good") is a Jewish name, and its bearer had married into an influential Jewish family that gave him personal links with some of Jerusalem's top people, including Eliashib the high priest, whose son had married Sanballat's daughter (6:17–19; 13:3–5). Tobiah's son, too, had married into Israel's aristocracy. Evidently the top people regarded Tobiah as one of themselves and resented Nehemiah's negative attitude toward him (see 6:17–19). Yet Tobiah, "the Ammonite official" (2:10)—that is, the Jew who had made Ammon "his chosen sphere, in which he had gained high office"—had ganged up with Sanballat in regretting, scorning, and opposing the reconstruction of Jerusalem's walls. . . . He was a worldly-wise formalist and pragmatist, hard-hearted as well as hard-headed, who was not so foolish as to let his faith affect his personal or professional life. To him also the glory of God as a motive meant precisely nothing. He was a cynic, of a kind quite familiar in the modern world.

What of "Geshem the Arab" (2:19)? Writes Kidner: "There is evidence that Geshem (cf. 6:1ff), far from being a negligible alien, was an even more powerful figure than his companions. . . . From other sources it emerges that Geshem and his son ruled a league of Arabian tribes which took control of Moab and Edom."[2]

Packer goes on to tellingly say, "In local churches and parachurch bodies, any leader who values order above ardor and routine above revival, and who pours cold water on visionaries as soon as they propose something be done, risks becoming a new Sanballat or Tobiah."[3]

It is important to realize that Nehemiah and his fellow believers were surrounded physically on every side by opposition, with the only means of escape the sea to the west. But Nehemiah was not dissuaded by opposition, as the early builders of the Second Temple were, nor was he surprised by it. He was not distracted by it either, nor should we be.

Nehemiah was confident that they as a people were seeking to obey the will of God and that they would therefore have his help. He would grant them success, as he was behind their project, and they would get on with the task they had been called to do without allowing any interference (2:20). This clear-sighted leadership and commitment by the people meant that, by God's grace and help, the job would get done.

13

The Family of God at Work

NEHEMIAH 3:1–32

MOST OF WHAT I HAVE written about the list in Ezra 2 could be repeated here about this list, with one big difference. The former list is about the identity and distinctiveness of the people of God, whereas this list is about church family cooperation and collaboration in getting the work of God done. It is an "all hands on deck" kind of chapter, celebrating the effectiveness of the church "when each part is working properly" (Ephesians 4:16).

Nehemiah was no slouch, and this chapter shows his brilliant organization of willing hands in forty-five sections of the wall. The chapter shows "all the marks of shared enthusiasm."[1]

We ought to note again the importance of the lists of names in Scripture, despite the difficulty of publicly reading them. They remind us of three important truths:

- These are real people. God is acting in redemption and restoration in history.
- Individuals who serve God may be forgotten in secular history and may never have a mention there. But they are remembered by God and are valued in the records of Heaven.
- Often chapters full of names are a bit off-putting, but they are part of God's revealed truth given to teach us, and they will reward study just like every difficult part of Holy Scripture.

Your life can count for eternity (or not). What legacy will you leave behind? As we go through the chapter we will notice four important principles.

Not All the Work Is Equally Distributed,
but All Workers Are Equally Responsible

Some had more work to do than others: "Baruch son of Zabbai zealously repaired another section" (3:20, NIV; "vigorously repaired"[2]). It is true that in church life generally the 30/70 rule applies—often 30 percent of the congregation does 70 percent of the work, and also of the giving. Some will always do more than others, but if everyone else at least plays their part as best they can, that will prevent some from overwork and will bring joy to all concerned.

Not All the Work Is Equally Pleasant, but It All Is Equally Important

The wall is only as strong as the weakest link, and it all needs to be built well, including the difficult parts. It cannot have been easy in the heat to be assigned to the restoration of the Dung Gate (3:14), which was called by its name for a reason. Some Christians only want the limelight jobs, but remember, the preacher will have a more difficult time if the heating has not been turned on or the pews/seats have not been dusted.

It is also important that people pull together rather than each one doing his or her own thing. I remember a well-intentioned person who decided on her own to varnish all the pews in our church without telling anyone. The next Sunday was the hottest in the year, and people left church with unwanted stripes of varnish on their white shirts and dresses.

I also remember working with a staff team member who was solid gold. Nothing was ever too much trouble for him, and he was always willing to at least have a go at things needing to be done, even when they were outside his comfort zone. What a great example he was to us all!

Not All Workers Are Equally Gifted, but All Are Equally Valuable

Goldsmiths and perfume makers (3:8) might have preferred working in a cleaner and more comfortable setting, but some were willing to get their hands dirty and discover other gifts in the process. As they caught the vision, they were willing to take risks in regard to what they would attempt to do.

When I was in my late teens I used to help with an open-air witness. I remember the minister saying to me, "After the next hymn, please give your testimony." I was a shy teenager and protested that I couldn't do that. He replied, "Jesus was publicly crucified for you, and you are unwilling to publicly speak up for him." That convinced me to go ahead and speak, and I experienced surprising liberty and a deep sense of God's peace and presence, and this in turn confirmed my call to the ministry, with which I had been struggling. I don't recommend this as the right tactic for everyone, but I needed a push to be willing to see what gifts God had actually given to me.

Like the believers in Nehemiah's time, we need to serve God with our strengths, working together like any good team and being willing to move out of our comfort zones in order to serve the Lord.

Not All Workers Are Equally Enthusiastic (3:20), but All Work Repays Personal Investment (3:28)

This was sheer genius on Nehemiah's part. Where possible, people built the walls where they lived. This not only made it handy to zip home for a sandwich or whatever, but there was a vested interest in defending one's own family. Serving God and doing his work is always in the best interests of your family. Putting God first enables us to see our responsibilities more clearly as a father, mother, son, or daughter (also as an employer/employee) and to get things straight and put in the right order.

Notice that the high priest and his fellow priests took the lead (3:1), working side by side with the craftsmen, artisans, and men of trade. "The fact that they consecrated their portion of the work emphasized the nature of the whole enterprise."[3] Especially take note of how often "next to him" or "after him" is mentioned in this chapter, too often to reference. The whole project was a collaborative effort.

Once when speaking to the first battalion of the Coldstream Guards, I was deeply moved by the fact that when the believers in the regiment gathered together to pray beforehand with their commanding officer, there were no ranks as we knelt on the floor to ask God's blessing, though on the parade ground there were ranks.

This chapter in Nehemiah displays the amazing family of the church. Old and young, skilled and not so skilled, all have a part to play to honor God and further his kingdom. There are up-front people and behind-the-scenes people. The church is where barriers are broken down. Even "daughters" joined in the manual work, which would not have been expected (3:12).

Years ago the rock band Pink Floyd complained about being just another brick in the wall, but God's people know that he is building a church of "living stones" into "a spiritual house" through his Son and for his glory (1 Peter 2:5).

Notice two other things:

Some leaders felt themselves to be above the work because of pride, but the rest simply got on with the work (3:5). There were also leaders who were not so proud (3:14).

There are a number of Meshullam's in Ezra—Nehemiah. If the Meshullam mentioned in verse 4 is the same person mentioned in Ezra 10:15 as an opponent of Ezra when Ezra sought to encourage the people to live by God's Word and commands, then here in Nehemiah he has been forgiven, restored, and is helping with the work. Whatever our past, God can forgive and restore us and use us to his glory!

This chapter should encourage every Christian to rejoice in the grace of God that has brought us into his glorious and eternal family. But it should also encourage us to ask if we know what our gifts are. If you are not sure, pray and ask a trusted friend or leader what gifts he might have observed in you. Also, be willing to take a risk in trying some service opportunities in order to discover gifts you never knew you had.

Also, what part are you playing in the life of your church? Are you casual in your commitment, or are you playing your part as you should? Some Christians suffer from what a friend of mine called "notionalism"— that is, having plenty of ideas for others to do rather than being willing to say, "Here I am, Lord, use me!"

A New Testament Perspective

The New Testament echoes the thoughts in Nehemiah 3: "Only let your manner of life be worthy of the gospel of Christ, so that whether I come and see you or am absent, I may hear of you that you are standing firm in one spirit, with one mind striving side by side for the faith of the gospel, and not frightened in anything by your opponents" (Philippians 1:27–28).

14

Getting the Work Completed

NEHEMIAH 4—7:4

IN OUR STUDY OF Nehemiah 1, we began to look at the answer to the important question, How does the work of God get done? and saw that Nehemiah laid down foundational principles for that to happen. We also saw how Nehemiah shared the vision with people in Jerusalem and started the work on the wall. The situation has now moved on (cf. 4:6 with 6:15). The passages we will examine now describe what happened to get the job done. Here is a strategy for finishing the work.

This is probably where most Bible-believing churches are. Good things have been done, but there is more to do. A work for God can start enthusiastically but falter halfway through. Nehemiah 4—7 will help us endure for work well done.

If you read Ezra and Nehemiah consecutively, you will no doubt have a sense of deja vu when you get to these chapters as they parallel the opposition that the Jewish people faced in rebuilding the temple (Ezra 4—7). As the people of God set about the work God had called them to do, opposition mounted. The book of Ezra makes the important point that this opposition will reappear in different ways in each generation; we must expect it and by God's grace overcome it. Nehemiah's point is equally important: the opposition can get very intense indeed, but with God's help we can overcome that too.

Notice how opposition mounted as the people of God set about the task and refused to give up.

From Outside

We have seen before how the Jews were surrounded on the north, east, and south, with the sea to the west. Now another hostile group from the west, the Ashdodites, is mentioned to complete the circle (4:7).

The initial setting for the jeering of the work probably was a military parade in Samaria, perhaps even within sight of some of the people in Jerusalem, where Sanballat's political friend reviewed the strength of the army and was the main speaker at the parade (4:1–3). Tobiah clearly considered himself to be something of a wit, so he cracked a corny joke at the expense of the builders. The escalating opposition started with ridicule, which had its effect (4:4) in seeking to wear down and discourage the builders. This was followed by physical threats and intimidation in a saber-rattling exercise and plotting together to prevent the work from progressing any further by causing fear and confusion about what was going to happen (4:7–8). When this did not work as intended, an invitation to an ecumenical peacemaking negotiation was politely pressed (6:2, 4–5). But Nehemiah discerned that this was a hindrance to getting God's work done, due in part to the geography, as the suggested meeting place was near hostile territory (6:2b). We need to remember that Sanballat was on the fringe of the Old Testament church, and Tobiah was a Jewish name—he would have been what we might call today a nominal church member.

Such pressure can be discouraging and upsetting. I remember a fine and godly lay elder telling me of a conversation he'd had at work that week. He and his colleagues were talking on a Monday about what they had done the previous weekend. He said he had attended an excellent men's breakfast on Saturday followed by an equally good Harvest Supper on Saturday evening. What with services on Sunday, he said that he had spent a lot of time at church over the weekend and that he and his family had had a wonderful and enjoyable time. His gentle, pleasant witness was met with the rather unpleasant remark from his closest colleague, "You must be mad!" He was shocked by the hostility but not put off.

From Inside

The New Testament reminds us that it is possible to "grow weary of doing good" (Galatians 6:9; 2 Thessalonians 3:13) and to become "weary or faint-hearted" (Hebrews 12:3). This happens more easily when we are physically exhausted, as the builders of the wall were becoming (4:10). They were involved in a huge and heavy task, and the effect of the psychological warfare was telling on them too (4:11). They felt the pressure of being the minority, and they desperately needed encouragement, but instead were being told by their friends to quit (4:12). "It's dangerous for you to stick your neck out for God like this. Just come home and live a quiet life."

From Economic Problems

The people were also facing severe economic problems that were affecting their families (5:1–5). As if the job was not challenging enough, there was a famine (5:3b) to cope with, and their Jewish landlords were showing no mercy, exacting high interest on their loans (or perhaps seizing assets because of inability to pay rent and repay loans). The background to this is Leviticus 25:35–43 and the requirement to help a poor Jewish brother and not to charge him interest on a loan or allow him to end up in slavery. But this was precisely what was happening to the people in Nehemiah's time. Some of their daughters had already become slaves, and others were in danger of going the same way (5:5). This callous behavior of fellow Jewish landlords was outrageous, and mothers and fathers rightly protested (5:1). Such behavior was clearly contrary to God's stated commands.

Nehemiah was justly angry that the nobles and officials were behaving in this way, and he knew that something had to be done about it right away. The suffering and injustice were real and required immediate action. This serious internal problem would prevent the people from completing the task that God had called them to do, and the whole resettlement in Jerusalem and Judah would suffer as a result. When Nehemiah's anger had cooled down, he brought charges against the nobles and the officials (5:6–8a). When confronted with the problem, the accused were speechless and had no defense (5:8b). So Nehemiah said, "The thing that you are doing is not good. Ought you not to walk in the fear of our God to prevent the taunts of the nations our enemies?" (5:9).

They were not living in a way that respected God and his commands, and that was an appalling witness to unbelievers. Nehemiah saw that he and his servants were implicated also, and his solution was to stop the taking of interest altogether, and for the nobles to do this too and also restore any confiscated property to the people (5:10–11). Convicted about their bad behavior, the nobles agreed and said, "We will restore these and require nothing from them" (5:12).

Nehemiah knew that it was possible to be sorry but not repent and put right a wrong action; so he made them promise in the presence of the priests as sacred witnesses (5:12a). He also, in a dramatic action reminiscent of the prophets, shook out the folds of his garment as a warning of God's judgment if they did not repent and change their ways (5:13). In those days, garments were loose with plenty of folds of extra material held together by a belt. Thus the folds acted as pockets, and for them to be shaken out meant the landlords would be judged and dispossessed if they did not keep their promise (5:13a). All the people said, "Amen" ("Surely" or "So be it"), "and the people did as they had promised" (5:13b). Obedience to God's Law brought resolution and settlement, and the people had a heart to worship and thank the Lord.

Because the taxes had been heavy on the people in time of need, Nehemiah, whom we are now told had been appointed earlier as governor by the king, never in his twelve years in that role claimed the food allowance that would normally have been allocated for the governor from the taxes (5:14). He never claimed his due despite the large daily demands to feed some 150 people. Nehemiah was clearly not doing the work for his own profit; rather, his action spoke of a labor of love for God and his people (5:14–19; cf. the Apostle Paul's comments in 1 Corinthians 9).

From Attempts to Undermine the Leadership

Two tactics were used to frighten the people into stopping the work. First, the fifth request to Nehemiah from Sanballat to "take counsel together" (6:5, 7) took the form of an open letter for all to see and contained a potentially dangerous accusation which, if believed, would have prompted the king to intervene with military might. The accusation was spelled out in what might have been a believable rumor, had it been true: "And according to these reports you wish to become their king. And you have also set up prophets to proclaim concerning you in Jerusalem, 'There is a king in Judah'" (6:6–7). To do this would have been to overstep his role as governor, and Nehemiah was quick to deny what was a fabrication: "No such things as you say have been done, for you are inventing them out of your own mind" (6:8). Nehemiah told the truth and prayed that God would overrule the intentions of Israel's enemies and help him finish the task without Persian intervention (6:9).

Second, Nehemiah was warned by Shemaiah, a seemingly concerned man with an apparent spiritual pedigree, that his life was in danger and was urged to take refuge in the temple (6:10). This was backed up by others (6:12) and seemed plausible enough. But Nehemiah saw through this advice, as it would have necessitated his disobeying the Word of God, which forbade anyone but priests to go into the sanctuary (Numbers 18:7). If he had entered the sanctuary in a moment of understandable panic, he would have faced serious punishment. Though his position as governor might have prevented such a consequence, it would have led to his being seriously discredited among the people. His opponents had plotted this "so they could give me a bad name in order to taunt me" (6:13). The Hebrew here is strong and shows that they really wanted Nehemiah's leadership to be rejected. His answer was a clear-headed one, by a man who knew the Scriptures and his own place in God's plan for his people.

Nehemiah answered, "Should such a man as I run away? And what man such as I could go into the temple [to save his life, ESV margin] and live? I will not go in" (6:11). Nehemiah knew that vengeance belongs to God (Deuteronomy 32:35). So he left Shemaiah, Noadiah, and the others who tried to make him afraid and discredit him in the hands of the Lord, who would deal with them in judgment (6:14). "With the help of our God" the people refused to be hindered in the work, and they got the job done in spite of the undercurrent of unhelpful and complaining letters that continued (6:16–19).

How can we apply all this today as we seek to live for God and fulfill his will for us in our day and generation? A friend of mine once described the basic problem of the church in the West as essentially one of "a loss of nerve," fearing an unbelieving world that seems so big and powerful in its influence. A little while ago a survey was done in Manchester, England. Eighty percent of young adults in their twenties said they would go to a Christian event if invited by a Christian friend. However, 70 percent of young committed Christians were afraid to ask their friends to such an event. The problem in evangelism has more to do with us than with the world. We have a glorious gospel to proclaim that is the answer to humankind's deepest needs. Why should we be fearful? You are probably well aware of some of the excuses we sometimes use. Here are just two:

- *The problems are too great!* Serving Christ can sometimes be tough and challenging, and it is easy to become weary in doing good, especially if plodding on in a difficult harvest field. But joyful obedience brings reward and fruitfulness in affecting lives for eternity, which is far superior to the sad feeling of having wasted good years.
- *What about me and my needs?* The soul-destroying, me-centered nature of modern society is self-absorbed and apathetic toward the needs of others and hostile to a caring society and a healthy church. God knows all our needs, as distinct from our wants, and it is only as we put him first that we find true fulfillment and the reason for which we were made, as well as being able to order our lives in a responsible and helpful way.

If the job was to be done, Nehemiah knew there needed to be three key ingredients. Let's look at each in turn.

Prayer

I love the comment of Charles Swindoll that Nehemiah was a "leader from the knees up!" Right through the book he is seen praying and encouraging others to pray. He had learned well the lesson of the importance of prayer in the months he had prayed in Susa for God to intervene and do something to restore and bless his people against all human odds.

He prayed on his own, and the people of God prayed too (4:4, 9; 6:9 where "O God" is implied). His first instinct was to pray, not to do. Ours is too often the other way around; we plan or do something and then ask God to bless it.

The sharpness of his prayer that their enemies receive their comeuppance (4:4–5) certainly does not model a Christian model of forgiveness, but two things need to be said to put it in context. First, note that Nehemiah left any vengeance or judgment to God. Second, Nehemiah saw the opposition they were all experiencing as opposition to God himself and his purposes, and therefore it was extremely serious (4:5).

Partnership

Nehemiah 4:6 tells us that the wall was already half built because "the people had a mind to work," or as the NLT puts it, "the people had worked with enthusiasm." It was an impossible job and would have remained an incomplete vision unless everyone played their part. But they had responded well to the task and to the enemies' challenges.

They Pulled Together (4:6)

We see the people united in their task and pulling together. We should all seek to fulfill the advice of Paul to live a life "worthy" of the gospel, "eager to maintain the unity of the Spirit in the bond of peace" (Ephesians 4:1–3).

They Prepared (4:9, 13)

When Oliver Cromwell addressed his soldiers, he in essence told them, "Trust in God and keep your powder dry." The people of Israel took responsible action to safeguard against the threats. Nehemiah placed guards on duty at the most vulnerable places of the wall where the wall was most accessible.

They Planned (4:16–17, 20)

They appear to have taken shifts in turn to hold the weapons and to do the work (4:16, 21). "And each of the builders had his sword strapped at his side while he built" (4:18). Nehemiah also organized a trumpet alarm system to rally people together where needed during an attack (4:20). The builders also remained in Jerusalem so that there might be a 24/7 guard on the walls (4:22). They never put their weapons down even when they went to get a drink or to freshen up (4:23; see ESV margin). Furthermore, Nehemiah wisely stationed them with their families and in their clans (4:13).

They Played to Their Strengths

On a good baseball team, where each person plays his part, the captain might not be the top pitcher or the hitter with the highest batting average but will nevertheless have a key role to play. Under Nehemiah's leadership, the Jews practiced this principle as well (4:15–16; see also Nehemiah 3).

They Were Pliable and Willing to Be Led

The people listened and obeyed Nehemiah as their leader, and they all shared the same vision and determination not to be distracted but to get the job done. Contrast this with a fine pastor and dear friend of mine who once shared with me the difficulty of being the senior minister in the church he was serving: "I have too many managers in the congregation who all have their own ideas as to how to run the church. We are a church full of chiefs, without many willing workers to do the work."

The church in Nehemiah's day kept at the work God had called them to do. They were watchful, and they were committed to the fellowship (4:9, 20).

Perspective

Above all, they kept a clear view of God before them (4:14b, 20; 6:9, 16). They were encouraged to do what they could, looking to God for his help and trusting him to be with them and keep his covenant promises through it all. Nehemiah knew that "unless the LORD builds the house, those who build it labor in vain. Unless the LORD watches over the city, the watchman stays awake in vain" (Psalm 127:1–2). Above all else, he knew that the success of the mission depended on God's providential working on their behalf.

Nehemiah was always telling the people in essence, "Keep your eyes on God. He is bigger than your problems. See what he has done and what he will help you do." He encouraged them not to look at the rubble and the size of the task, but to look up to God who had called them to the work and who would help them get it done. In whatever we seek to do for the Lord, according to his will, we need that perspective too. The following is an apt and challenging comment: "Of all biblical characters, Nehemiah is perhaps the most explicit on 'the practice of the presence of God.'"[1]

When I was growing up in southern Ireland, we lived near what I call a proper pointy mountain called Sugarloaf. I loved that mountain; it always dominated my horizon and brought me perspective. When I awoke in the morning and pulled back the curtains, it was there. When I went to school and went out into the playground, it was there in the background too. When I went to the beach with my friends for a swim, there it was, looking down on us again. In a spiritual sense we need to always keep God on our horizon and rejoice in his steadfast love toward his redeemed people.

Despite all the jeers, threats, and opposition, the wall was built in record time, and the gates were rebuilt as the final part of the complete restoration of the structure (6:15; 7:1). The finished work was a great witness to their surrounding neighbors. They saw it never would have been done without God's help (6:16), and therefore their own cocky, anti-God self-reliance was dealt a considerable blow. "For the faithful, the measure of success that they experienced could only be traced to the Lord's help and enablement. God's providential provision was also evident in the failure of all the attempts to frustrate the work or to interfere with its progress. Nothing had prospered against the work for one very good reason—the Lord had prevented it."[2]

It is important to remember that the building of the walls was a means to an end—establishing a community that worshiped God and gave him his rightful place in their personal, family, and community lives (7:1). This explains the responsibility and the tribute given to Hananiah, seeing that he was "a more faithful and God-fearing man than many" (7:2). The sensible arrangements for the opening and closing of the city gates, for reasons of safety and security, would have encouraged the sparse population to feel more secure and to carry on as normal (7:3–4).

New Testament Perspectives

We see a New Testament equivalent in the Apostle Paul's words, "I thank my God in all my remembrance of you, always in every prayer of mine for you all making my prayer with joy, because of your partnership in the gospel from the first day until now" (Philippians 1:3–5). Like the people of Israel in Nehemiah's day, the Philippian believers were exceptional in their practical and prayerful gospel partnership with Paul (Philippians 4:15). Furthermore, the writer to the Hebrews reminds us of the need to "obey your leaders and submit to them, for they are keeping watch over your souls, as those who will have to give an account. Let them do this with joy and not with groaning, for that would be of no advantage to you" (Hebrews 13:17).

Also like the Jews who rebuilt the wall, New Testament believers need to rely on God to help them accomplish their God-given task.

> Finally, be strong in the Lord and in the strength of his might. Put on the whole armor of God, that you may be able to stand against the schemes of the devil . . . praying at all times in the Spirit, with all prayer and supplication. To that end keep alert with all perseverance. (Ephesians 6:10–18)

This side of Heaven, God's people are involved in a spiritual battle, but God supplies the strength and equipment to see us through. The Lord is with us on every step of our journey.

15

The Importance
of Continuity

NEHEMIAH 7:5-73a

THIS CHAPTER LARGELY REPEATS the list of names in Ezra 2. The interest in this chapter is not just due to the minor differences in the numbers, all of which can be accounted for in different ways—for example, by the subsequent inclusion of latecomers returning with the first exiles.[1] The interest lies in the reason Nehemiah thought it important to rehearse the original list of returning exiles at this point.

The answer lies in the word *continuity*. It was important for the wall builders to remember who they were—the current expression of the people with whom God had graciously entered into a covenant of love and mercy—and that they were in continuity with the covenant people of God from ninety years before. They needed reminding of their identity and why they were there. The list also reminded them of the courage and sacrifice of the first generation of returning exiles and challenged them to have the same commitment.

Note Nehemiah's words: "*My* God put it into my heart to assemble the nobles and the officials and the people to be enrolled by genealogy" (7:5). This verse displays the intimate personal relationship Nehemiah had with God, just as David had when he wrote, "The LORD is *my* shepherd" (Psalm 23:1), and that Paul had when he wrote, "I live by faith in the Son of God, who loved me and gave himself for *me*" (Galatians 2:20). This God, Nehemiah knew, had prompted him to do what he was doing. God still prompts his servants today by his Spirit, but always only in ways consistent with the Word of God, which is our primary means of guidance. Those promptings can often be seen most clearly after the event has happened; it is clear then that God was in it.

So Nehemiah gathered the people to encourage them to see again who they were and that they must have the same concern to be obedient to God's Word as did the people in the time of Zerubbabel. There are important lessons from all of this for believers now. In our churches today there ought to be continuity of:

- *Worship*. The call to worship the living God whose grace and mercy we have experienced through Christ is essentially the same.
- *Doctrine*. Just as Nehemiah and Ezra were concerned that the people of God live by the Word of God (see Nehemiah 8), so today our commitment to the Word of God, including the apostolic doctrine of the New Testament Scriptures, must be the bedrock of our lives.
- *Fellowship*. When God saves his people today, he brings them into his church family with filial bonds of love between them, which we see reflected in the people of God in Nehemiah's time.

An apostle walking into one of our churches today should recognize the same direction and concern for worshiping the Father of our Lord Jesus Christ, the same teaching and doctrine that the apostles taught, and the same love for Christ and one another that stems from the experience of God's redeeming grace. Styles of dress, music, and culture change, but the substance must remain the same if we are to be faithful to God's revelation in Christ.

The fact that some churches drift from this commitment is a matter of deep regret and, if serious enough, disqualifies them from being recognizable Christian churches at all, no matter what is on the church sign. Continuity is profoundly important.

Continuity is also important because it involves passing on the faith by example, teaching and loving our children and our children's children. This is expressed wonderfully in Psalm 78:4–8:

We will not hide them [the teachings they had received] from their children,
    but tell to the coming generation
the glorious deeds of the LORD, and his might,
    and the wonders that he has done.

He established a testimony in Jacob
    and appointed a law in Israel,
which he commanded our fathers
    to teach to their children,
that the next generation might know them,

the children yet unborn,
and arise and tell them to their children,
   so that they should set their hope in God
and not forget the works of God,
   but keep his commandments;
and that they should not be like their fathers,
   a stubborn and rebellious generation,
a generation whose heart was not steadfast,
   whose spirit was not faithful to God.

The Jews of old knew their responsibility in this regard, and so should we. The prime responsibility for handing on our faith to a new generation is with us as parents and grandparents. This may be greatly helped by good youth leaders in a gospel church, but we must not abdicate our responsibility.

It is clearly important that, as in the book of Nehemiah, an awareness of church history and the exploits and examples of previous generations of believers is taught. Furthermore, as the true children of Abraham, inheriting the promises to him by faith through Christ, we have generations of Biblical examples to learn from (cf. Hebrews 11).

Note also that the generosity of the original leaders was repeated in order to spur the current generation to the same generosity and sacrificial giving in response to such a generous God (7:70–72).

New Testament Perspective

We who are the beneficiaries of the new covenant should be even more eager in our response to such a generous God.

> But you have come to Mount Zion and to the city of the living God, the heavenly Jerusalem, and to innumerable angels in festal gathering, and to the assembly of the firstborn who are enrolled in heaven, and to God, the judge of all, and to the spirits of the righteous made perfect, and to Jesus, the mediator of a new covenant, and to the sprinkled blood that speaks a better word than the blood of Abel . . .
>
> Therefore let us be grateful for receiving a kingdom that cannot be shaken, and thus let us offer to God acceptable worship, with reverence and awe, for our God is a consuming fire. (Hebrews 12:22–24, 28–29)

16

Revival

NEHEMIAH 7:73b—8:18

THIS MARVELOUS PASSAGE TELLS us about the sovereign activity of God in bringing revival and reformation to the church in Nehemiah's time, affecting the whole nation of Israel for good. In the words of David Jackman (in a sermon I heard), what was happening here was "the Spirit of God taking the Word of God and creating the Community of God."

Nehemiah knew that the building of the walls was a means to an end—the restoration of Jerusalem as a safe and secure place to live, in order that God's people might worship and serve him, enjoy his presence with them, and be a light to the nations. But the walls were of no use without the Word of God being the central guiding force in their lives. Living by the promises of God, enjoying a covenant relationship with him, and seeking to obey his commands as his grateful redeemed ones constitutes normal living for the people of God.

Clearly the gathering had been planned and was expected to take place because a platform had already been built (8:4). The people wanted to meet and were of one mind in doing so (8:1). Just days after returning home from the building work, they gathered in the square near the Water Gate rather than at the temple, probably because of their numbers. Their motive was to keep the Feast of Trumpets (Leviticus 23:24–25), and their hearts were full of thanksgiving for all of God's gracious assistance and help in building the wall. "This goodness of God instinctively led them to hunger to hear from God's Word."[1] Here is described a Water Gate experience that transformed a nation, built them up, and brought joy, in marked contrast to the Watergate experience of the early 1970s in the United States that revealed an untrustworthy president and nearly brought a nation to its knees. The church here is seen to be in the marketplace, listening to God in a way that affected a city and a nation. The church of Nehemiah's day was experiencing God-sent revival and was seeking to be what it ought to be.

Four marks of a healthy church are clearly visible in this chapter.

The Church Gathered and Eager to Hear the Word of God

Just like at Horeb (in Deuteronomy 4:10, LXX, where we find the first use of the word *ekklesia* in the Old Testament), the people were gathered and were eager to hear what God had revealed through Moses. "And the ears of all the people were attentive to the Book of the Law" (8:3). They showed respect for the Holy Scriptures by standing as the book was opened (8:5), and they apparently remained standing for long periods of time (8:3).

Any ritual can lose its significance over time and become an empty ritual. I remember going to a service in Paisley Abbey in Scotland as a young man. The service began with a hymn and a procession, and leading the procession was a boy carrying an open Bible on a cushion. I was deeply moved as I saw that. The people standing in Nehemiah 8 was not a sign of bibliolatry but showed a desire to honor God and worship him by listening to his revealed Word. Attentiveness to the Word began in prayer and led to worship and praise of God (8:6). The people were eager not just to hear the Word but to understand what it meant, and they were teachable (8:8–9).

The Church Having the Highest Regard for Scripture

They understood that God had spoken to his people of old by revealing himself to Moses and that those Scriptures still spoke God's Word to them in their day and generation. Though Moses as author was the human agent, there was a deeper truth in his writings because of the Spirit of God's inspiration of the words; they were truly the words of God for them (8:14). The Scriptures they had were trustworthy and true because God had spoken his commands in this way. Also, as the New Testament reminds us, what God said he says still (Hebrews 3:7). "All Scripture is breathed out by God and profitable for teaching, for reproof, for correction, and for training in righteousness, that the man of God may be complete, equipped for every good work" (2 Timothy 3:16). The church at prayer in Acts showed the same respect for God's Word (Acts 4:24–28). In Old or New Testament times, a healthy church had the highest possible regard for the Holy Scriptures and sought to order and rule her life by them.

The Church Needing Faithful Preachers

Although the exact details of how they did this are unclear, what is crystal clear is that Ezra and his friends understood that the deepest need of the people was to hear God's Word read and to have it explained to them so that they understood it (8:8). What appears to have happened is that Ezra with his thirteen friends read the Scriptures in turn and in sections from early morning (6 A.M. approximately) until midday (8:3–4), and the thirteen Levites went throughout the crowd explaining the meaning of what had been read (8:7–8) so that everyone understood.[2]

The word translated "clearly" in verse 8 could be translated in a number of ways. It could just mean "distinctly and articulately" read or, perhaps more likely, "translated" since many of the people spoke Aramaic rather than Hebrew. More likely still is "with interpretation" (see ESV footnote). Perhaps the best idea is to combine the last two meanings. The Levites as they moved among the crowd were translating and interpreting so that "they gave the sense, so that the people understood the reading" (8:8). They clearly expounded and applied the Word of God to a people eager to hear, which notably included men, women, and children old enough to understand (8:3).

All this is in marked contrast to what happens in too many congregations in the West today, where the Word of God is read poorly and without adequate preparation or training, and its reading is limited to just a few verses. In many churches the preaching also can be largely theme-centered or topically focused. Though this can be helpful on some occasions, this passage makes it abundantly clear that preaching properly is the exposition and application of Holy Scripture. This is what God's people need and should want. If the Bible is not faithfully taught and expounded, the people of God are shortchanged. The Bible is not a resource book from which to dig out our favorite ideas. It is the treasure of the Word of the living God, given to us to be taught, grasped, understood, and taken to heart through faithful expository preaching, with the help of and in the power of the Holy Spirit. May that be true among us, and may God raise up many faithful preachers. As Paul told the Ephesian elders, "I did not shrink from declaring to you the whole counsel of God" (Acts 20:27).

The Church Discovering That Obedience to the Word Brings Joy

As we shall later see more fully, the first effect of the Word of God read and preached is that the people begin to understand just how great the Lord is, how wonderful has been his redeeming love to them, and just how faithfully his steadfast love has been with them over the years. As they see God afresh as he really is, they see their own sinfulness and how they have not deserved the least of his mercies. They begin to weep in mourning for their own sinfulness, and also with joy because of God's incredible covenantal goodness and kindness to them over the years (8:9). A deep, not superficial, God-induced emotional response was healthy and right as they responded to God's Word. But Ezra knew that the people needed to be directed toward the joy of the forgiveness that God brings to those who truly repent and believe in his mercy and grace. The people were no doubt tired by now, as well as being emotionally moved and drained. So Ezra and the Levites sent them to eat, celebrate, and share their resources with those less able to do so, with the great truth that "the joy of the LORD is your strength" ringing in their ears (8:10). The Levites calmed down the crowd rather than whipping them up into further emotion and sent them on their way rejoicing that they had heard, understood, and responded to the Word of God (8:11–12). How much wiser and what a contrast that is to some emotionally driven services and rallies today.

We need to think a little bit more about the statement "the joy of the LORD is your strength" (8:10). The word translated "strength" can have the meaning of refuge or protection. The point of this verse is that they had been protected from the deserved consequences of their disobedience to God's Law by the covenant mercy of the God who loved them and had forgiven them. This was the ground of their joy and the cause of their great rejoicing. Today the undeserved grace of God shown to us in the forgiveness won by the atoning work of Christ on our behalf and the further blessing of God adopting us into his family and "bless[ing] us in Christ with every spiritual blessing in the heavenly places" (Ephesians 1:3) should be a constant source of joy to us.

On the day following this great gathering, the heads of the families and the spiritual leaders—all who had a special responsibility to see that the Word of God was taught and understood by the people—met for further Bible study with Ezra (8:13). Ezra was clearly respected by both Nehemiah and the people as a fine Bible teacher, and the crowd had asked for his ministry the previous day (8:1). As the leaders studied with him, they discovered that in this crowning seventh month of the year, God had commanded that his people celebrate the "The Feast of Booths/Tabernacles" from the fifteenth day of the month until the twenty-second day (Leviticus 23:33–43). This had been neglected since Joshua's day (though see Ezra 3:4), but it now became a source of "very great rejoicing" (8:17c) as all the people camped out on this joyful family occasion. No doubt the children loved the idea of going camping with their family and friends. The feast was a harvest celebration and a reminder that during the difficult days of the wilderness wanderings, God had protected and provided for them, and now once again he had brought them back to their promised land. Once the discovery was made of God's command, which required obedience but which God intended for their blessing, they had just two weeks to let everyone know and get prepared (8:14–18). During that time God's Word continued to be read by Ezra each day (Deuteronomy 31:10–13), and the week-long event ended with "a solemn assembly" on the eighth day (8:18). They no doubt also observed the Day of Atonement on the tenth day of the month, though that is not mentioned by the writer here.

So discovering what the Scriptures taught and obeying its commands brought new joy to the whole community. It is always like that. There is nothing better as a believer than knowing that you are doing the right thing because you are obeying God's Word. However challenging that may be at times, it will always bring real joy in its wake.

It is important to realize that if the previous points are marks of a healthy church that God is blessing and renewing, then the opposite are marks of an unhealthy church that is resisting the blessing of God. Let us now consider obstacles to revival happening in the church.

A Lack of Conviction about the Trustworthiness of God's Word

Liberal theological skepticism has seriously infiltrated many theological institutions in the West for many generations now. It has undermined ministerial confidence in the Holy Scriptures, has created congregations that are ill-informed about their faith, and has led to serious decline in numbers attending church. One particular form of this is to make much of reader response theory, the claim that the Scriptures only mean what they mean to me (rather than asking what the author originally meant and, consistent with that, what it should mean to us now in the light of God's full revelation to us in Christ). As we all disagree about the Bible's meaning, so the argument goes, we can no longer trust what it says. The church in many places has effectively abandoned the authority of the Bible and replaced it with the authority of personal experience. It has failed also to uphold the Reformation doctrine of the perspicuity (or clarity) of Scripture in all things necessary for salvation, which has led to confusion about first-order theological issues as well as an inability to evaluate and withstand the politically correct views of our time. On the other hand, the historic doctrine of the inerrancy and infallibility of Holy Scripture, historically as well as theologically, and its essential clarity on all things that really matter, has consistently brought conviction, clarity, and health (cf. 8:14ff.) when believed and put into practice in the church.

Impatience with Serious Study

The spirit of the age encourages us to abandon anything that is demanding or hard. We prefer instant results. But every athlete who achieves anything knows that success comes only after months of training and discipline. Study of the Scriptures daily and weekly brings great benefit. As Paul put it to Timothy, "Train yourself for godliness; for while bodily training is of some value, godliness is of value in every way, as it holds promise for the present life and also for the life to come" (1 Timothy 4:7).

The people here, and the leaders especially, gave themselves to the study of the Law (8:13), and that brought a new godliness as well as great joy and blessing (8:12, 17). We need to become people of the Book again (this once described England and the early colonies in America, but sadly this is no longer true).

An Unwillingness to Be Holy and Distinct as God's People

Pressure from the world, the flesh, and the devil has often led to the people of God not living in a way that brings attention to our Savior and glory to his name. Surveys show that Christians in the West are often no different than the people among whom we live and to whom we are called to witness. We are meant to be lights that point to the Light of the world. When we ape the world in our church decisions and personal lifestyles, we fail to be what we were meant to be. The people in Nehemiah's day were willing to be distinct and different in obedience to God's claim upon their lives (9:2–3).

Hesitancy about Letting the Word of God Challenge Our Traditions and Practices

Traditions are healthy when they reflect apostolic doctrine and teaching (see, e.g., 1 Corinthians 11:2; 2 Thessalonians 2:15; 3:6). Unhelpful traditions can be five years old, or fifty, or five hundred or more.

When I was a minister in a church that was turning in an evangelical direction, a woman complained about me introducing a monthly Holy Communion service in the evening when all our different congregations could come together for fellowship. Though there was a regular early morning Communion, she complained about having this service in the evening because when she was confirmed as a teenager, the bishop had said that people should come to Communion fasting and in the morning. I reminded her that Jesus instituted the Lord's Supper in the context of a meal and in the evening, so it must therefore be alright. She thought for a minute and then said, "But the bishop said it should be in the morning without breakfast!" We sometimes base our security in the practices we are used to rather than in the Lord and the teaching of his Word. As the Reformers rightly emphasized, the church should be *semper reformanda*, that is, always reforming itself by the Word of God and with the help of the Holy Spirit. The people in Nehemiah's day showed a willingness to change their ways as they discovered what the Scriptures taught (8:14—9:3).

Application for Today

This wonderful chapter gives us insight into the way in which God revived his church in Nehemiah's day, and this pattern has always been true in times of revival in the history of the church of Jesus Christ. A God-sent revival is desperately needed again in our day and generation, especially in the West. Every touch of God in personal revival and in the life of our local church should make us long for this to happen more widely and deeply in a way that affects whole nations. May we catch the vision by looking over Nehemiah's shoulder and praying and working for the church to be like what we see in Nehemiah 8 (or for that matter, in Acts 2). In all of this we need to remember how easily we slip away from best practices as Christians and churches and how merciful God is to us.

17

Recounting the Goodness of God

NEHEMIAH 9:1-37

SEVERAL THINGS ARE NOTABLE about this chapter as we begin. Firstly, there was only a short time between the end of the Feast of Booths and this assembly on the twenty-fourth day of the seventh month. Possibly only one full day to rush home and change or just stay put with a day off from the proceedings. The people were serious about their response to God. Secondly, while Nehemiah had not wanted the convicted people to wallow in their sins but rather to rejoice in God's goodness in protecting them from deserved judgment (8:10), he had also wanted them to see that God's way is good and that obedience to his commands brings joy and blessing (8:17). But the people had unfinished business with God; they needed to confess their sin and cast themselves on God's mercy. They also needed to show a repentant spirit by consecrating themselves to obey the terms of the covenant with a new seriousness. So they gathered for a service of confession and rededication. Their seriousness is seen in their attitude as they came to worship "with fasting and in sackcloth, and with earth on their heads" (9:1). They also realized in a fresh way that they were meant to be a holy people set apart to worship and serve the Lord. So they "separated themselves from all foreigners" who had not joined them (cf. Ezra 6:21) and "confessed their sins and the iniquities of their fathers" (9:2).

It is important to notice that it was the reading and exposition of God's Word (9:3) that recounted to them the goodness of their God and the depth of their and their fathers' sins down the generations. Only as we see God in his greatness, love, and mercy do we truly see what we are like. This is an important truth, as we will never see our sin properly without the revelation of God's character and grace. This should affect how we order our Sunday worship services, an essential part of which must include recounting the goodness of God as his Word is read and preached and as we reflect on God's grace and goodness to us, his redeemed people. It is only as we see God that we truly see ourselves and deep praise wells up in our hearts and expresses itself in lips that delight to worship God in praise and with surrendered lives.

The service here consisted of three hours of reading, understanding, and taking to heart God's Law and three hours of confession and worship. The Levites, made up of two overlapping groups presumably standing on the stairs of the platform (8:4; 9:4), led the people in either confession or praise (9:5). The prayer seems to have begun at verse 5b rather than just being led by Ezra (see ESV footnote for 9:6).

Central to the people's hope was the nature of the God they served. That nature is marvelously expressed in the two central verses of this chapter (9:17, 32). But note throughout their prayer all that they affirmed about the Lord, who is "exalted above all blessing and praise" (9:5). They recounted the goodness of God in the following ways:

He is the creator and preserver of all, which includes not only the earth and all that is in it, but the highest heaven and the angelic "host"(or army) (9:6). It is important in our day, when we are often removed from the land in urban or suburban settings and when atheism shouts that there is no God, to remind our congregations that our Savior is also our Creator to whom we owe life and loyalty. The world does not exist by time and chance, but was created by a good and loving God who is working out his purposes. He is not here today and gone tomorrow, but is "from everlasting to everlasting" (9:5). Recognition of this truth reminds supermarket shoppers that without the God-given soil, sun, and rain, there would be no food to buy.

This mighty God of creation is also the one who has chosen to enter into a covenant relationship with a people for his own glory and their benefit (9:8). The Lord chose Abraham, whose name change is a play on words reminding him of God's promise to make him "the father of a multitude of nations" (Genesis 17:4–5; Nehemiah 9:7–8).

He became his people's redeemer, delivering them from slavery in Egypt in such a powerful and unforgettable way that "you made a name for yourself, as it is to this day" (9:10). The memory of that deliverance was hardwired into his people down the generations. That act of love and mercy had made them who they were as his redeemed people (9:9–11).

He did not just deliver them and leave them to their own devices, but guided them through the wilderness and revealed to them his will for their lives, the way of joy and blessing. In every way, spiritually and materially, he had provided for their needs on their journey (9:12–15). His love for them was steadfast and sure (9:17).

That dependable love was seen in his unwillingness to give up on them when they refused to listen to him and rebelled against him. He still guided them by day and night, his Spirit was present with them, and he sustained them and provided for their every need through forty years in the wilderness (9:16–21).

He prospered them and gave them a home and a kingdom as he promised, enabling them to possess the delightful land as their inheritance by military victories (9:22–25). As they took possession of the land, they grew in numbers and thrived.

He persisted in loving them and in being committed to them even when, though enjoying the blessings of a fruitful land, they continued to rebel. He warned them, and when they refused to listen, he gave them into the hand of their enemies to discipline them; but when they repented and cried out to him, he restored them. Though they richly deserved to be abandoned by God, he never gave up on them because he is "a gracious and merciful God" (9:26–31).

Retracing and Facing the History of Their Sinfulness

This recounting of the sheer goodness of God threw into sharp relief their persistent sinfulness through the generations that they now confessed with a heavy heart and painful honesty. They and their fathers before them had acted "presumptuously," taking advantage of God's favor and refusing to listen to God's Word, casting it behind their backs (9:16, 26, 29). By casting God's Word aside, they were actually casting God aside (see 1 Kings 14:9). The catalog of their sin makes sad reading, as they had failed to understand that God knew what was best for them and had their interests at heart, and that to follow him and his ways and laws was the way to real life (9:29). The cycle of blessing, rebellion, distress, restoration, rebellion, blessing, distress . . . was repeated throughout their history (9:16, 26, 28–30). The people's evaluation of this history was that God's grace and mercy had been consistent throughout (9:31) and whenever he had judged his people, it had been just and deserved (9:33). So this prayer is one of heartfelt repentance and a desire to be different in the future with God's help (9:38).

Realizing Their (and Our) Only Hope

As they recounted the character of the God who had entered by grace into a covenant relationship with them, they became aware in a fresh way of their own sinful unworthiness of his steadfast love, which in turn led them to be sorry and repent of their personal and national sinfulness. It is not sin that is our ultimate problem but the holiness of a just God whom we must one day face. True as that is, it is the very character of God that gives us hope—indeed our only hope! In this chapter, two magnificent passages describe just how wonderful our God is:

- "But you are a God ready to forgive, gracious and merciful, slow to anger and abounding in steadfast love, and did not forsake them" (9:17b).
- "Nevertheless, in your great mercies you did not make an end of them or forsake them, for you are a gracious and merciful God" (9:31).

I love the contrast in this chapter between the "but they" in stiff-necked and presumptuous rebellion (9:16) and the "but you" of God's gracious willingness to forgive and show mercy (9:17b).

New Testament Perspective

This all reminds me of my two favorite words in the New Testament found in Ephesians:

> *But God*, being rich in mercy, because of the great love with which he loved us, even when we were dead in our trespasses, made us alive together with Christ—by grace you have been saved—and raised us up with him and seated us with him in the heavenly places in Christ Jesus, so that in the coming ages he might show the immeasurable riches of his grace in kindness toward us in Christ Jesus. For by grace you have been saved through faith (Ephesians 2:4–8a).

We are sinners just like the Jews of old, rebels in God's world who richly deserve his just judgment. But when we repent and believe in the provision made by God's unique Son for our forgiveness by his substitutionary death for us on Calvary's tree, taking the punishment that was ours by right, we are forgiven and restored into a relationship with God as his beloved children. This happens by the grace and mercy of God. Those who say the God of the Old Testament is a God of wrath and the God of the New Testament is a God of love have simply not read the Old Testament properly. The Bible is one book that testifies thankfully to a God of justice *and* love, whose purposes of redemptive mercy and grace were worked out for his repentant people by the death and resurrection of the Lord Jesus Christ. All who come to him find forgiveness, love, and restoration.

It is to this God of mercy and grace, "our God, the great, the mighty, and the awesome God, who keeps covenant and steadfast love" (9:32), that God's people in Nehemiah's day appealed. In essence they prayed, "Lord, have mercy. Because of our sins we have suffered much. Please realize that and see that we are in trouble. Though you have graciously brought us home, we are still slaves in the land of promise, paying heavy taxes to a foreign king. Please show us yet further mercy and grace." It was to God's steadfast covenant love they appealed, with a heartfelt desire to amend their ways and keep their covenant obligations as his people. The scene is now set for the renewing of the covenant in the next chapter of Nehemiah and an ongoing experience of the God of grace and mercy in their lives.

When we see God as he truly is, not only do we become aware of our own sinfulness but we become aware of God's willingness to save and forgive. While the Scripture-based revelation of God's majesty and holiness becomes the means of exposing our true need, it also reveals the mercy and grace of the only One who can meet our deepest need. When we experience that grace through Spirit-given repentance and faith, we have a source of endless hope and joy and a reason to praise God with all our hearts.

"The ultimate test of our spirituality is the measure of our amazement at the grace of God. . . . The measure of our spirituality is the amount of praise and thanksgiving in our prayer."[1]

18

Renewing the Covenant

NEHEMIAH 9:38—10:39

I HAVE FOR SOME time thought that the yearly Methodist Covenant Service, often taking place around New Year's Day, was a good idea. When well prepared for, and if focused on the gospel of grace, it gives believers an opportunity to thank God for all his goodness to them and to renew their commitment to him as their Lord and Savior (see the excellent prayer at the end of this chapter). While normal Christian living is love for and daily obedience and commitment to the Lord Jesus Christ, it is good from time to time in a special service to renew our response to the call of our gracious covenant-making God on our lives.

The Jews of Nehemiah's day understood the value of this at such a critical point in their lives. Indeed, the renewal of the covenant had been a pattern at key times in their past history. As they were here taking their covenant obligations seriously, and since they clearly could not all literally sign up in ink, they wanted their commitment signed by their leaders (9:38); hence the list at the beginning of Nehemiah 10.

Nehemiah and Zedekiah were uniquely joined together by the word "and," setting them apart as key civic leaders. The rest of the list was comprised of priests and Levites, often described in terms of their family, as well as "the chiefs of the people" (10:14). Ezra's name was not mentioned, as he was included prominently in the family group "Seraiah" (10:2). Six or seven of the Levites mentioned here were among the teaching group that helped Ezra (8:7).

There is a strong sense in these lists in Nehemiah of collective responsibility and support for one another in the serious business of expressing real repentance in practical action. At the same time the nature of the lists, mentioning specific names, reminds us of personal responsibility and also of God's care for his people not only collectively but individually. As well as the signatories, "the rest of the people," including the children old enough to understand, joined in the renewal of promises and commitment (10:28–29). In the light of the reading of the Law—no doubt including "You shall be holy to me, for I the LORD am holy and have separated you from the peoples, that you should be mine" (Leviticus 20:26)—they took their calling to holiness seriously (10:28). This centered around their commitment "to walk in God's Law that was given by Moses the servant of God, and to observe and do all the commandments of the LORD our Lord and his rules and his statutes" (10:29). They had a real desire to be practically obedient, and they were aware of the consequences of gross disobedience.

Several areas of practical importance in their situation were singled out, in addition to their general commitment, out of gratitude for God's continuing grace to them. Desiring to do God's revealed will for their lives as his redeemed people, they made several promises.

Not to intermarry with the people around them (10:30). This was not a racial issue, as we have seen, but a religious one. Such intermarriage brought pagan influences into their family life (Exodus 34:12–16). In that sense, mixed marriages are always unwise, and this applies to Christians too (2 Corinthians 6:14–18).

To keep the Sabbath. This would affect their work and trading arrangements (10:31). They would also keep the seventh year as specified in the Law (Exodus 23:10–11). The following quote is helpful: "God certifies his covenant by signs: for the covenant with Abraham, circumcision (Genesis 17:11); with Israel at Sinai, Sabbaths (Exodus 31:13, 17); with Christ and new Israel, the cup (Luke 22:20)."[1]

The Sabbath was of special importance to a people wanting to renew the Mosaic covenant, and what an appropriate sign and blessing it was! With the challenge of daily work and faithfully walking in God's good ways, what a blessing a day of rest, refreshment, and worship could be! God knows when we need a break and cares deeply for our welfare. "Not neglect[ing] the house of our God" (10:39) involved three obligations:

- *They gave yearly "for all the work of the house of our God" (10:33b).* This was a third of a shekel, which was less than stipulated in Exodus 30:11–16 and less than the New Testament practice of half a shekel (Matthew 17:24, 27), but probably all the people could afford at the time. Rebuilding the temple was the first and foremost reason for the exiles to

19

Recreating Community

NEHEMIAH 11

CREATING A SENSE OF COMMUNITY in a village, church, or nation is important, as we will see in this chapter of Nehemiah (see 1 Chronicles 9 for more details). Nehemiah was seeking to do what he could to further community spirit. Jerusalem was called "the holy city" (11:18) and was both central to the purposes of God for his people and essential as the capital city for the well-being of the nation as a whole. Though its walls were now built, bringing security, it was underpopulated, and therefore its security would be short-lived if there were not enough people to defend it. Furthermore, its security was only the first step in a return to normality with rebuilt houses and businesses being established or reestablished.

Nehemiah encouraged the necessary steps to help restore Jerusalem to its former glory and healthy economic operation. While the key leaders and some others lived in the city, the aim was to get one in ten of the population living in the city (11:1). So lots were drawn to see who would move from the outlying villages into the city. It appears that some volunteered to move, and the whole community saw the value of all this and was grateful for those who moved sacrificially and willingly to reestablish the city (11:2). "Strange as it may seem, it was a real sacrifice for some people to come and build a house and settle in Jerusalem. Some were drawn by lot, while others offered themselves willingly (11:1, 2)."[1]

When Jerusalem had been undefended, people had become used to living in the country, and it was a sacrifice for many to give up their home and farms and move to the city, the rehabilitation of which presented a considerable challenge. The enemies of the Jews, while tolerant of a scattered population, also feared the establishment of a strong rival city and a clear reestablishment of national life that the health of Jerusalem would provide. "Today some prefer the country, others prefer city life, and while it is often possible to have the one that we prefer, we must remember that the service of God overrides any special locality."[2] An overriding concern for the well-being of the whole community needed to be foremost in the people's thinking.

When I was the senior minister in a large (by English standards) suburban London church, we had an interesting issue to resolve. We had two identical morning services to accommodate everyone, but we needed more time for fellowship between the services so that the preaching especially would not be unduly pressured time-wise. Our deacons were united in seeking to address the issue. The question was, Which service needed to move by fifteen minutes to make this possible? Would the 9:30 service move back to 9:15, or would the 11:00 service move to 11:15? After lengthy discussion, we voted; eleven voted one way and twelve the other. Being the good people that they were they said, "We have made a decision. Let's live with that!" I said I did not think it was good to be divided on such an issue and asked them to go away for a month, ask their home group what they thought, lay aside their own preferences, consider what was best for the church as a whole, and above all pray each day about the matter so that the right decision would be made. The result exceeded my expectation. We made a unanimous decision a month later (with one abstention—there is always one). The first service moved to 9:15.

We had made huge decisions before about important issues, but in a time-conscious society dominated by London Underground schedules that influenced people's getting to work each day, this relatively secondary issue had divided us. The effect on our church council thereafter was considerable. Whenever we seriously disagreed on an issue, someone would say, 'Let's pray more about this, lay aside our own agendas, and prayerfully consider what is best for the church." That by God's grace was community spirit growing happily and healthily. Churches are too often dominated by selfish agendas or dominant individuals who lack a servant spirit or a willingness to accommodate others when possible. We learn an important lesson from Israel of old in this chapter that will bring health to church life today.

New Testament Perspectives

When we turn to the New Testament, we see the best motivation for the creation of church community spirit:

> I therefore, a prisoner for the Lord, urge you to walk in a manner worthy
> of the calling to which you have been called, with all humility and gentle-

ness, with patience, bearing with one another in love, eager to maintain the unity of the Spirit in the bond of peace. There is one body and one Spirit. (Ephesians 4:1–4)

How do we maintain our God-given spiritual unity as true believers (Ephesians 4:3)? By humility, gentleness, and patience (Ephesians 4:2), by thinking of others first. This is the servant-hearted mind of Christ (Philippians 2:4ff.). Timothy was a good example of following the example of Christ (Philippians 2:19–22). So were Prisca and Aquila, that tremendous couple who moved home and country to support Paul in his work and to establish a local church that Paul had founded (Romans 16:3).

I have traveled around a lot as a preacher and bishop. Too many churches lack this kind of community spirit. Some churches may be good at an initial welcome but are still hard to get into as they are cliquish and not on the lookout for new folks or outsiders. We fail to influence many with the gospel by not adequately addressing this issue.

Nehemiah was a good leader, and he knew that the community spirit so evident when they were building the wall had to be maintained in order to establish the church community now that the greatest threat of danger had probably passed. So he did what he could to foster that spirit so that the renewal of the church community was complete. God moved in the hearts of his people to be willing to sacrifice for the well-being of the church.

The list in the rest of the chapter reveals to us an ordered society. They were aware of who they were as God's people and were clear about what needed to be done. "Valiant men" (11:6, sometimes translated "men of substance") and "mighty men of valor" (11:14) were useful in defending the city. The whole picture (filled out in more detail in 1 Chronicles 9) gives us a sense of everyone playing their part, like an orchestra working together to produce beautiful music. Their central driving force was clearly around the worship of the temple and thankfulness to the God of grace who was helping them and using them in the restoration of his church (11:17). Provision was made for the singers (11:23), and the Levites had "chiefs" and "overseers" appointed over them to make sure their tasks were done (11:16, 22). Even the king far away had a commissioner report to him what was happening in the Jewish community (11:24).

In summary, the work of God and good organization, with a God-centered focus to build his church and glorify his name, are not enemies but friends! One of the gifts of the Holy Spirit is being literally a helmsman, being able to steer a ship, translated as "administrating" (1 Corinthians 12:28). Good leadership is a God-given gift to his church.

20

A Joyful Celebration and a New Beginning

NEHEMIAH 12

MANY TIMES IN CONNECTION with my calling, I have been to and taken part in a dedication/consecration of a new church building or hall or the completion of a worthwhile project that was now ready to be opened and used by the community. Those are always times of great delight and joy, and any setbacks or difficulties and perhaps the costly sacrifice of many are soon overwhelmed by a desire to thank God for all his help from beginning to end. There is also always a desire that God bless the work. People need reminding that God's blessing on the use of this or that is desperately needed, for "unless the Lord builds the house, those who build it labor in vain" (Psalm 127:1). A place of ministry for God is not built for the glory of the builders (though they deserve thanks) but for the glory of God and the extension of his kingdom. We should never be like a church I have heard about that spent millions on a new church center but then was afraid to let the mums and toddlers group use it in case they marked it or spoiled it.

This chapter, full of praise and thanksgiving, marking a job well done, begins with a list. Why? As we have seen before, continuity is important. The people of God here were the restored community, the heirs of the covenant to Abraham and Moses. They stood in continuity in a special covenantal relationship with God, whose obligations they had just recommitted themselves to keep as God's redeemed people. One of the striking things in this chapter is the repeated comment that the worship and praise at this celebration in "the city of David" (12:37) was in line with the directions of "David the man of God" whose musical and liturgical practice they were seeking to emulate (12:24, 36, 45). As we will see in a moment, there was fresh joy and praise, but they were not seeking to be novel.

"The title 'man of God' marks David as one regarded by the community as having unusual stature and authority, particularly with regard to music and liturgy. . . . The use of similar language in describing David and Moses may hint at an implied comparison between the two leaders *par excellence* in ancient Israel."[1]

The list then speaks of continuity, with family names being used and kept down the generations, and passages of time being marked out by the "reign" of the high priest at the time (in the absence of a king's reign to mark out succeeding generations) (12:1, 22). Note verses 10–11, of which it can be said:

> This bridges the gap between the first generation after the exile (the period of vs 1–9) and the contemporaries of Nehemiah. It carries forward the genealogy of I Chronicles 6:3–15, which ran from Aaron to the Babylonian exile; and like that document, which omits some names known to us from other scriptures, it does not necessarily include every generation. Between Jeshua, who returned from Babylon in 538, and Eliashib, the high priest in Nehemiah's time about a century later, Joiakim (v 10) may not have been the only link in the chain, though it is not impossible.[2]

Note that the names in verse 24 have also been mentioned as signatories to the renewed covenant commitments in Nehemiah 10.

The Dedication of the Wall (12:27–43)

This was marked by both organized and spontaneous praise and thanksgiving. The two great processions with the two choirs in the lead would have taken some organization. One started in the south and went counterclockwise, and the other in the north went around the other side of the wall. What memories the people would have had as they passed the bit of the wall they had worked on and as they viewed the completed whole (12:31, 38)!

But the emphasis on joyful and spontaneous praise to God is seen by the fact that they met together at the temple to worship, praising God for all that he had done for them over the years in bringing them back to the promised land, helping them build and refurbish the temple, and enabling them to build the walls of "the city of David" so that the whole national community might be renewed and revived. They had not only built the walls but repented deeply for past sin and put matters right with the God of grace whose unfailing, steadfast love to them filled them with joy and delight. They made a loud, joyful noise to the Lord, their praise even being heard far away (12:43).

The Hebrew word *toda*, meaning "thanksgiving" (12:27), refers to thanksgiving songs of a personal or communal nature, as in many of the Psalms.

> Such songs are characterized first and foremost by their exuberant praise of God and their acknowledgment of the benefits that he has rendered, whether to the community as a whole or to the individual in particular. . . . The object of the word . . . is properly God and not human beings. . . . The word suggests spontaneity and cheerfulness, rather than mandatory and required. . . . The word "toda" thus suggests thanksgiving in the form of praise rendered to God in public acknowledgment of his help provided in prior times of desperation.[3]

This was not superficial worship but was undertaken with both heartfelt praise and seriousness, as the ritual purification of verse 30 shows. The term used is a reminder that all sin, of whatever kind, has no part in the life of the people of God and must be dealt with by the means of grace that God has provided.

This chapter is not only a delightful description of a great national day of celebration for the church, but it marked for the community a whole new chapter, a new beginning, as they sought to live in grateful obedience to the Word of the God to whom they owed their very existence!

Service at the Temple (12:44–47)

It is probably more helpful to translate verse 44a as "at that time." Nehemiah was no slouch as a leader, and he was aware of the people's delight in having a secure temple as the focus of God's promised presence with them and their delight in and appreciation of the ministry carried out there (12:44). So he made sure that the promise "not [to] neglect the house of our God" (10:39) was properly organized for a practical outcome and that the Levites as well as the whole ministry team were not neglected (12:44, 47).

New Testament Perspective

It is worth remembering that in New Testament times, those who teach us the Word of God and minister to us need to be practically appreciated too (Hebrews 13:7, 17). How much real appreciation is shown to those who minister in our congregation? Do we pray for them regularly and responsibly support and care for them as best we can?

How heartfelt and exuberant is your praise and that of the congregation you belong to each Sunday? How great is God's steadfast love to us in Christ, and how worthy he is of all our praise!

21

Broken Promises

NEHEMIAH 13

WE MIGHT WISH THAT the book of Nehemiah ended at 13:3. So much had happened that was encouraging. God's people had known God's power in revival, and the future looked bright. Which one of us would not cry out, "Lord, may the church of my day know this sort of blessing, this sort of revival and renewal!" Do we not long for this in our secular and materialistic age in the West? So much had been put right in the life of the church and the nation, and it all revolved around obedience to the Word of God that was once again shaping their community and national life and was bringing them blessing as a result (13:1–3).

But chapter 13 shows us the need for ongoing reformation and renewal. Hard-won spiritual victories can be rapidly lost. This chapter describes a post-revival situation in desperate need of a fresh touch from God. It has been rightly said that the great truths of God's Word need to be fought for afresh in each generation. Nehemiah had been governor for twelve years, and during this time all seemed to be well. But now he had returned to Susa, and in his absence, things began to fall apart. We do not know how long he was away before he returned, but on his return he found that the promises made in the renewing of the covenant in chapter 10 had been seriously and dangerously broken. Nehemiah was angry with what he found.

As the phrase "On that day" (13:1) is somewhat indefinite, it is probably best to take 13:1–3 along with 12:44–47 as a description of how things were when Nehemiah returned to Susa and spent some time with the Persian king. Things had been going very well when he left Jerusalem, but while he was absent, standards declined and the people became disobedient to God's Word again. Had the leadership that Nehemiah left behind not really been up to the task? Perhaps, but the people had the leadership they deserved as the blessings of revival became a pale memory.

Reformation and revival always need to be ongoing—*semper reformanda*. Good leaders like Nehemiah understand that persistence in obedience to God's will and ways demands vigilance in every generation. When he returned, he did all he could to rectify the declining spiritual situation, a situation which caused him great sadness. The spiritual decline described by the book of Malachi seems to fit into this time.

The Problems He Found on His Return

The problems were threefold and are mentioned in reverse order compared with the same problems mentioned in chapter 10.

The *first* problem had been brewing for some time. Social and family ties had kept Tobiah's influence going among the nobles (6:17–19). Now this opponent of the work of the Lord had gained a foothold in the temple itself. While Nehemiah was away, Eliashib the priest (the high priest, 13:28, and related to Tobiah) had given Tobiah a large storeroom in the temple as an apartment for the time he wished to spend in Jerusalem. "There Tobiah could oppose God's work while posing to assist it."[1] This was specifically against God's command that no Ammonite should have a place in the temple, and it was rightly understood as "evil" by Nehemiah on his return (13:7). He consequently threw all the belongings of Tobiah out of the chamber, cleansed it, and restored it to its former use. This was important, as it was a storehouse to keep the provisions that enabled the Levites to go about their work, and until Nehemiah restored things, they were not being adequately provided for. Many had returned home to their land in order to survive. The whole temple operation, despite earlier best intentions, was grinding to a halt, for it seems the people had been slack in these provisions also, making the situation for the Levites even worse (13:10). Bad leadership and a poor sense of responsibility among the people had made life hard indeed for the Levites (despite the people's earlier enthusiasm for Levitical ministry, 12:44).

The three very areas in which the people had promised to be obedient to God when they renewed the terms of their covenant obligations in chapter 10 were the very things they failed to do! Their previous covenant promises had ended with the solemn promise "We will not neglect the house of our God" (10:39). But that is precisely what they were now doing, and Nehemiah reminded them of that (13:11). So again, driven by obedience to God's Word as the right and best way for the people to live, Nehemiah sorted out the lack of provision for the Levites, called the people to provide the promised tithe, and put reliable people in charge of the practical running of the temple organization (13:10–14). As the temple was central to the healthy life of a worshiping community, it is not surprising to find that this whole section begins and ends with concerns about the temple and its personnel. Nehemiah found that not only had Tobiah gained influence in the temple courts but Sanballat also had influence through a daughter's intermarriage with a grandson of the high priest (13:28). Nehemiah's conclusion was vivid and clear: "They have desecrated the priesthood and the covenant of the priesthood and the Levites" (13:29). So he did what was necessary to purify the priesthood and see that the temple was working again in a godly and well-organized way (13:30–31).

The *second* problem that needed reforming was the need to purify the Sabbath and keep it holy to the Lord. Greed had eroded godly business practice, and pressure from pagan traders was making it difficult as well. Again Nehemiah had both the courage and authority to sort this further "evil" out. So he confronted the nobles and reminded them that this self-same problem of profaning the Sabbath had previously provoked God's righteous anger (13:15–18). He also dealt practically and forcefully with the pressure from pagan business interests and put the Levites, who had purified themselves, in charge of guarding the city gates on the Sabbath (13:19–22).

The *third* problem that needed to be addressed was purification from mixed marriages with non-Jewish neighbors (13:23–27). Nehemiah saw this intermarriage with unbelieving foreign women as "act[ing] treacherously against our God" (13:27). "The issue at stake for him was preservation of religious purity, which could only be assured by maintaining use of the sacred language."[2] How could children influenced particularly by their mother's culture, brought up not knowing Hebrew, know and enjoy God's blessings or be obedient to his Word (13:23)? Within a generation the distinctiveness of God's people and their ability to fulfill their divine mission would be jeopardized or lost. While Nehemiah did not seem to advocate the abandonment of such marriages, as had Ezra, he made the people promise to stop the practice, and he made his opposition to the practice strongly and forcibly known (13:25).

The comment of Matthew Henry is helpful: "Ezra, in this case, had plucked off his own hair, in holy sorrow for the sin; Nehemiah plucked off their hair, in holy indignation at the sinners. See the different tempers of wise, and good, and useful men, and the divers graces, as well as divers gifts, of the same Spirit."[3] We might add that the work of the Spirit in the new covenant situation does not require that we follow Nehemiah's example in this respect, even if we keep hold of his right concerns about believers marrying unbelievers.

We find ourselves as believers today fighting a battle against the values of a world in rebellion against its Maker and seeking to squash us into its mold. Strong external pressures hostile to God and his ways, if yielded to, can weaken or render ineffective the life and witness of Christians and the church. The words of H. G. M. Williamson are an important warning: "The Christian Church continues to face these issues, albeit in different forms. The principles for appropriate response remain the same: a strong core of leadership and a clear line of demarcation at the fringes. From a position of strength and security it is possible to extend a hand of welcome and forgiveness to those outside. From a position of weakness both parties would sink together."[4]

It is a wonderful thing that God, when seeking to revive his church at this time, gave them two leaders—one essentially a man of the Word (Ezra) and the other essentially a man of prayer (Nehemiah). Both of these are at the heart of every reviving touch of God. Prayerful, joyful dependence on the promises of God in a new way and a heartfelt, thankful desire to obey God's Word are evidence of every genuine reviving and renewing work of God. God uses his Word and prayer to revive, renew, and reform his church.

Ezra and Nehemiah are, in the words of J. A. Motyer, "two of the most attractive characters that the Old Testament offers,"[5] and they are in so many ways examples to us. As the meanings of these names suggest, God *helped* (Ezra) and *comforted* (Nehemiah) his people through God-enabled leadership.

Two Questions for Us

What are we to make of Nehemiah's thrice-mentioned appeal to God in this chapter to remember him and all he has done "according to the greatness of your steadfast love" (13:22; 13:14, 31)? Nehemiah had committed himself to the cause of God, and in asking to be remembered, he was asking for God's help and intervention. He was also, in the helpful words of Derek Kidner, wanting to hear God's "Well done," which is "the most innocent and most cleansing of ambitions."[6] God does not forget service done out of love for him.

A second question is, Did Ezra and Nehemiah fail? Once again the words of J. A. Motyer are helpful: Ezra "saw a problem and settled it scripturally. We must not read Ezra 10 with hindsight from Nehemiah 13 and conclude that since the problem re-emerged Ezra failed. Rather, we should affirm his success in that it did not need to be readdressed for another quarter of a century, and then, apparently, in a much more limited form."[7] The same could be said for Nehemiah. The people's stumbling in disobedience does not mean that

Nehemiah failed. Under the hand of God, he brought revival, and when that needed further renewal upon his return from Susa, he was not found wanting but persevered as a godly leader with a passion to call God's people back to obedience to God's Word with a real, repentant heart.

After a particularly pleasing result one weekend, I discovered that the rugby team I support (Leinster Rugby, based in Dublin) was so triumphant because of their "culture," according to one commentator. When asked what that was, he said it consisted of three things—humility, ruthlessness, and being brothers on the team together. It struck me that this was a good description of Nehemiah as a leader and a man of God.

- He was humble in his utter reliance on God to achieve his purposes. He always gave God the credit for what had been achieved because he knew that without his help, they would never have built the wall in record time or achieved anything else.
- He was ruthless in his determination, which never wavered, to call the people to repentance and faith in the promises of God and to live according to God's Word.
- Though a strong leader, he did not place himself in a lordly way above his brother believers and always identified with them—the "we" passages—and led them as part of a band of brothers (and sisters).

We have much to thank God for in the ministry and example of Nehemiah. May God give us Nehemiah's heart for the glory of God and the health of his church!

———

A review of Nehemiah is now helpful.

Leadership Lessons from Nehemiah

"Nehemiah had the skills of a great leader. We can learn from him again and again in this area. But even more important was his deep dependence on God, and we can learn from that too."[8] We learn several important lessons from Nehemiah's example.

1. Prayerfulness (1:4, 11; 2:4)
    - Consider also the examples of George Washington and Field Marshall Lord Montgomery as prayerful leaders.
    - "Nehemiah was a leader from the knees up!"[9]

- Nehemiah prayed with others also (1:11; 4:9).
2. Vision (2:7ff.)
    - He was willing to play his part and to sacrifice in order to be obedient to the Lord.
    - "He left the opulence of palatial surroundings for a dispirited community in a dilapidated city he had never known."[10]
    - Why? The grace of God had captured his heart (2:12).
3. Proper evaluation of the task (2:12–16)
    - He did this with a few trusted friends privately. This shows the need for having good people around you.
4. Sharing the vision (2:17–18)
    - He was humble: "we," "you see."
    - He gave encouragement (2:18). This shows the power of testimony.
5. Mobilizing the workers
    - They responded, "Let us rise up and build" (2:18).
    - Everyone has a part to play (Nehemiah 3).
    - He was willing to get his hands dirty.
6. The need for good organization (3—12)
    - "Nehemiah seems to have shortened the Eastern wall by keeping to the top of the ridge."[11]
7. Dealing effectively with problems
    - Outside (4:8–9, 13–14).
    - Inside (5:1–9). Nehemiah was a good example himself (5:14–15).
    - He kept perspective, keeping God in the picture (4:14; 5:9).
8. Value-driven projects (8—10)
    - God's Word gives us God's values. Obedience to God's Word brings joy.
    - They needed to make and keep promises (8:12; 10:29ff.).
9. Opportunities spotted and taken (12:44–47)
    - There was organization and oversight to help people keep their promises.
10. Review and discipline (13)
    - Things can slip.
    - We need to be careful who we leave in charge.
11. Commitment
    - A humble dependence on God, expressed in prayer.
    - Ruthless obedience to God's Word.
    - Being brothers and sisters together in a covenant community.

Some Final Thoughts on Nehemiah

I once sent a manuscript to a publisher who replied, "We like it, but it left us feeling we wanted a bit more!" Despite all that happened for good and blessing in the hundred years or so of the events described in Ezra and Nehemiah, one is left with a sense of disappointment and a longing for more; just as in the post-Easter church of the new covenant, there is a now and not yet element.

Not as many Jews returned from exile as had been expected, and this certainly fell short of the return of the whole nation. No Davidic kingdom was reestablished, and the people remained under the rule of pagan kings. Despite the manifold blessings for a time of the great revival of Nehemiah 8—10, the joyful obedience of the people faded, and the same old problems of disobedience emerged in the life of the church and nation. The promise of a new covenant that changes people's hearts was desperately needed.

> I will put my law within them, and I will write it on their hearts. And I will be their God, and they shall be my people. And no longer shall each one teach his neighbor and each his brother, saying, "Know the LORD," for they shall all know me, from the least of them to the greatest, declares the LORD. For I will forgive their iniquity, and I will remember their sin no more. (Jeremiah 31:33–34)

Clearly also, the messianic promises of Zechariah lay in the future:

> Rejoice greatly, O daughter of Zion!
> Shout aloud, O daughter of Jerusalem!
> Behold, your king is coming to you;
> righteous and having salvation is he,
> humble and mounted on a donkey,
> on a colt, the foal of a donkey . . .
> and he shall speak peace to the nations;
> his rule shall be from sea to sea,
> and from the River to the ends of the earth.
> As for you also, because of the blood of my covenant with you,
> I will set your prisoners free from the waterless pit. (Zechariah 9:9–11)

It was not until the coming of the Lord Jesus Christ to Jerusalem on Palm Sunday that this promise was fulfilled, and it was not until he graced the temple precincts with his royal presence that the glory of the Lord once again came to his temple.

Both of these promises of God, as yet unfulfilled, as well as the people's need of a deeper work of God in their hearts, cried out for the coming of our Savior, Jesus Christ. So the last books of the Old Testament leave us expecting and longing for the promised Messiah to come. What a good way for the Old Testament to end—it pointed to the glorious fulfillment of the purposes of God in the coming to earth of his precious Son to live among us, and supremely to go to the cross for us as our sin-bearer and substitute, and to rise again to open

Heaven to us! Ezra and Nehemiah show us sinners our need of Jesus' atoning work and point forward to what he achieved for us! Here are two wonderful choruses that express this truth so well:

> Out there amongst the hills
> My Saviour died;
> Pierced by those cruel nails,
> Was crucified.
> Lord Jesus, Thou has done
> All this for me,
> Henceforward I will live
> Only for Thee.
>
> —N. Shaxson[12]

> Wounded for me, wounded for me,
> There on the cross He was wounded for me;
> Gone my transgressions, and now I am free.
> All because Jesus was wounded for me.
>
> —William Gilbert Jones[13]

ESTHER

The Timeline of Esther

516 B.C.
Temple Rebuilt
(in Jerusalem)

478–473 B.C.
Events of Esther
(in Persia)

445 B.C.
Walls Rebuilt
(in Jerusalem)

22

The Selection of Esther as Queen

ESTHER 1—2

WE WILL EXAMINE CHAPTERS 1 and 2 of Esther together because they set the scene for discovering what the author wants to tell us. How on earth did a young Jewish girl become queen of Persia and subsequently be in a position to be God's agent in the deliverance of his people?

An apt title for the first section of the book of Esther could be "Men Behaving Badly," after the British TV series of the same name. The book begins with a party at which we see men behaving very badly indeed! But before we get into the details of Esther 1—2, some comments need to be made by way of introduction.

In the book of Esther the name of God is never mentioned. Some Jews were uncertain as to whether it should be included in the canon of Scripture because of that. Not only is the name of God never mentioned, prayer is never described (although I think there is a clue in one place about prayer, as we will see in our study of Esther 4). Worship is also never mentioned. Esther looks, on the surface, to be a secular sort of book. In the first seven centuries of the Christian church, no one wrote a commentary on the book of Esther. Neglecting the importance of this powerful little book is a serious error.

Also, in the situation being described here, there were some exiled Jews in Susa, the winter capital of the Persian empire, but this was a pagan environment. For those believers the question was, Where is God in our pagan world? Sometimes for us too it feels as if God is far away. It is one thing to feel God close when you meet with other believers, but what about the next morning in your office? Maybe for some, sadly, that is even what it feels like when you go home. What about your day-to-day situation? Where is God when he doesn't seem to be at work in your situation?

What we see here, I think, is a brilliant literary device used by the writer of the book of Esther. God is never mentioned by name. Nonetheless as we study the book, we discover that God is everywhere at work in every situation throughout the book. That in itself says a great deal.

As believers in a pagan world, we can sometimes wonder why God doesn't interrupt some things or break into some situations more obviously. We need to understand that God is at work behind the scenes of history. God is at work in the circumstances and muddle of life even when we are not aware of it. The writer of the book of Esther is telling us, in a clever way, that when it isn't obvious that God is there, he is! God is ruling and overruling in the circumstances of life. God is never mentioned anywhere in the book of Esther, but in a very real sense he is at work throughout it.

In his commentary on the book of Esther, Gordon McConville wrote, "The story can become therefore a powerful statement about the reality of God in a world from which He appears to be absent."[1]

I think the book of Esther is the greatest book in the Bible to teach the most underused word in modern Christian vocabulary. That word is *providence*, often neglected by modern Christians but not by evangelical Christians in previous generations. Among them, providence would have been highly valued and was common in their vocabulary. To grasp that God rules and over-rules in the circumstances of our lives for the good of his people whom he has redeemed, to bring glory to his name, brings sanity in the Christian life.

God works out his purposes in our world through all the mess, and he saves his people. No power on earth can hinder God's rule or keep his ultimate purpose from being fulfilled. We can trust God to work out his purposes for the good of the Church. As Paul put it at the end of Ephesians, "God placed all things under his feet and appointed him to be head over everything *for* the church" (1:22, NIV). Jesus Christ is Lord and exercises his rule for the benefit of the Church.

So despite what some think, the book of Esther is much more than an explanation of the Jewish feast of Purim—the feast of deliverance, at which Esther was (and still is) read yearly. It is a book that supremely teaches the providence of God.

Barry Webb's comments in his article on the book of Esther are helpful. "In particular, the hiddenness of God that we find in Esther mirrors the world many of us live in today, particularly in the West . . . the absence of the miraculous does not mean the absence of God." He goes on, "This message about the special Providence of God is one that is reiterated in the New Testament and one that God's people still—and perhaps especially—need to hear today (Romans 8:28)."[2]

The book of Esther is a marvelous book to teach us the critically important truth of the providence of God. It is a fabulous story brilliantly told. Karen Jobes, in her commentary on Esther, observes that because it is a story that hangs together so well, the book of Esther is difficult to preach.[3] Be that as it may, I've done it with profit and joy. It is a story that is meant to be read at one sitting; so if you are to understand this commentary, I would encourage you to read the whole book of Esther first (it's only ten chapters long). "This is not a book for bit-by-bit study, revealing its spiritual treasures best if you read it in one sitting."[4] It would be helpful to read it in a modern version, maybe in a more dynamic equivalent version than you would normally use for study (e.g., New Living Translation), as this kind of translation is helpful for reading narrative stories at one take. The book of Esther is history told as story, and brilliantly and dramatically done at that! Once you have grasped the story, you can look more carefully at the details.

Parties Bring Out the Worst in People

Bearing in mind those words of introduction, let us now consider the first couple of chapters. It won't surprise you that my first heading is that sometimes parties bring out the worst in people. In an unbelieving world, that is often true. People let their hair down (if they have any hair, speaking personally), and you often see their real priorities, motivations, and concerns. When people have eaten too much, and particularly have drunk too much, you discover what people are really like.

The opening chapter of the book of Esther describes a party to end all parties—it went on for six months (1:4)! Persian parties were especially famous, not so much for the food as for the drink provided (1:8). We are not told exactly how this was managed. It may be that all the military leaders, officials, and civic authorities in the vast Persian Empire (1:1) were invited in turn, progressively working through the list. Susa probably couldn't have coped with them all in one go. However it was managed, over a six-month period there was a tremendous party, which was also, it seems, the occasion for a council of war.

Historical Background

We know from secular history (Herodotus writing later in his *Histories*) that this party corresponded with an interesting circumstance. We are told by the writer of the book of Esther, who may have been Mordecai himself, that this mega-party occurred in the third year of the reign of Xerxes (the more familiar Greek name to us than Ahasuerus) (1:3). At that time he gathered together all the leaders of the empire and all the military figures to impress them with his power and pomp. In particular he wanted to drum up support for a military campaign against Greece and to show them that he could fund it and that he could also reward those who went with him. His father, Darius, had been defeated by Athens, and Xerxes—as the leader of the greatest empire of his day (the superpower of the ancient world)—clearly was more than a little annoyed that his father had been defeated by the Greeks. Xerxes was attempting to get everyone together to show them his power and the magnificence of his empire in order to drum up support for a mighty military effort against the Greeks, so he could teach them a lesson!

We know this was a disaster because Xerxes was famously beaten at the naval Battle of Salamis, his troops being delayed and harassed by just 300 Spartans led by King Leonidas, who with the help of other Greeks inflicted huge casualties on the Persian army at Thermopylae (480 B.C.). Four years later (2:16), when he came back from these wars, Esther became queen in place of Vashti. That was four years after the party of chapter 1, and it explains the delay in finding a replacement for Vashti: Xerxes had been away on his military campaign that spectacularly failed to avenge his father's defeat.

The Irony of the Situation

The situation opens in chapter 1 with all the nobles and leaders gathered together for this extraordinary feast, no doubt impressed with the pomp and power of Persia. But we understand that the writer of Esther would have written after the military outcome of the campaign was well known; with heavy irony he was showing us life behind the splendor, pomp, and circumstance of the greatest ruler of the known world. In spite of the splendor of the Persian Empire (here wonderfully described) and the promising nature of the war effort (Xerxes mustered a huge army), Xerxes and his armies were defeated, and he returned crestfallen and much the poorer. There was going to be failure in this huge war effort. Things were not going to turn out as planned.

There was also another pointed irony. Here we observe the Persian king, the king above all earthly kings, the superpower of the world of his day, unable to control his own wife. In displaying his power and rule, he asked his queen to come to the party and she refused. Things were not so good at home.

The heavy irony of the book of Esther draws back the curtain on events, enabling us to see behind the pride and the pomp sometimes evident in world affairs to show us a not-so-wonderful situation going on behind it all. What the writer is clearly saying to us, is, don't be dazzled by the power and pomp of the world that can seduce us or sometimes terrify us. Don't be afraid as a believer to be outnumbered and overwhelmed by secular and materialistic power. Things are not always as they seem, and we need to look behind the apparent circumstances of history to understand that sometimes the power and pomp is actually skin-deep. The writer was drawing back the curtain on a significant moment of history to show us life behind the scenes and with heavy irony describing the situation as it really was.

Right Behavior Doesn't Give Hangovers and Regrets

The book of Esther reminds us powerfully of the serious mistakes that we can make when we don't live in a way that is in accord with God's will and purpose. I have worked with young people a lot, and I have never understood those who have told me that a party at which you get absolutely drunk out of your mind, sick as a dog, and probably sick over someone else's floor, should be considered so much fun! You are left with a massive hangover the next day and may well wake up wondering what you did or didn't do the night before. How is that fun? But some people think it is. It may be for a short time, but the hangover and perhaps serious consequences have to be faced all too soon. The book of Esther warns us that when God calls us to act rightly and live well, that is for our blessing and the blessing of other people. Right behavior doesn't give us hangovers.

At the end of this period of indulgence the king invited probably all those officials who had organized the previous six months' festivities to the garden of the royal palace for a seven-day party (1:5, 10). And what a party! In certain parts of the world weddings can go on for days, but seven days?

> On the seventh day, when the heart of the king was merry with wine, he commanded . . . the seven eunuchs who served in the presence of King Ahasuerus [Xerxes], to bring Queen Vashti before the king with her royal crown, in order to show the peoples and the princes her beauty, for she was lovely to look at. But Queen Vashti refused to come at the king's command delivered by the eunuchs. At this the king became enraged, and his anger burned within him. (1:10–12)

The king "invited" the queen, who had been running a party for the women at the same time (1:9), to join them, and she refused. Xerxes had drunk too much. His command was foolish and probably felt by the queen to be demeaning. Vashti wouldn't play ball. I wonder if you have ever been at a party where there has been fun, but it all ended with bad feeling? This domestic incident put a damper on a huge civic party.

Vashti a Heroine?

Was Vashti a heroine or not? Some of the feminist commentators make Vashti out to be so (Vashti rather than Esther). They say she was refusing to be a sex object. She was especially admirable in her behavior, they say, as she resisted the unhelpful patriarchy of her day. Actually the book of Esther tells us what happened but doesn't comment too much on it. But it does describe the incident in a way that makes us have sympathy for Vashti. We think instinctively, *Good for her.* She was invited to a party, probably to be carried in on a litter by the seven eunuchs, her beauty paraded before a group of drunken men to satisfy the whim of her husband. Rightly she wouldn't play ball with the situation!

Some early Jewish commentators suggested she was invited to come along with her crown or headdress (v. 11) but nothing much else on. Other commentators have suggested that when we carefully consider the date of this party, she may have been pregnant with the king's son, Artaxerxes, and this of course would have added great weight to her resolve not to come along and be paraded. (This assumes that Vashti was another name for Amestris, whom Herodotus says was the queen mother of the future king.) Certainly it appears that she was right to refuse to come.

A Serious Domestic Situation Made Worse by Legislation

The king was so annoyed (he had lost face with the people he was seeking to convince of his authority) that he made it a legal issue and asked his advisers what to do (1:15). The mess they made of it is comic; they made a complete hash of it. Memucan shifted the domestic argument into a much wider issue. His reasoning ran thus: "If every woman in the empire discovers what the queen has done, we won't have a moment's peace at home! We have to do something about this in case the word gets out! We have to tell everybody in the whole empire that wives must respect their husbands or else!" (see 1:16–18). Some adviser! Who ever thought legislation could carry that one off! Also, what a ludicrous way to keep this news from getting around the empire—by telling everyone in the empire what happened and issuing a decree about it (1:22).

This was an overreaction by the king and his advisers. There is a reminder here that anger is a dangerous motive by which to take action. An old saying is, "Act in haste and repent at leisure," and so it was here. The situation described was really quite sad. Vashti was forbidden ever to see her husband again (1:19). Later on, when he returned from the war, "after these things, when the anger of king Ahasuerus had abated, he remembered Vashti and what she had done and what had been decreed against her" (2:1). In other words, he missed her and regretted what had happened. He regretted his action in anger. He regretted his overreaction and that of his advisers.

There is a word here for modern societies, including the ones in which we live. I think one of the notable things in Britain today is that there is a huge tendency to overlegislate. Why is that? When there isn't a moral consensus—that is, an aspiration to good behavior as summed up in the Ten Commandments—then government will end up overlegislating, trying to prescribe good behavior. We can't do that any more than the Persian Empire could legislate that all wives would respect their husbands, however badly those husbands behaved. The book of Esther portrays a king, that for all his power and authority, acted on a whim, was manipulated by his advisers, and afterward regretted what had taken place. With a ruler like that, Susa was a potentially dangerous place to live.

Winning Miss Persia and How Showbiz Can Go to Your Head

Esther, her Persian name, meant "a star" (her Jewish name was Hadassah, meaning "myrtle"). She won the ancient equivalent of a pop star talent contest in terms of popular adulation, except that it was more like winning a sexualized Miss World. Notice the movement in this chapter: she goes in one fell swoop from being a pretty orphan from an enslaved people brought up by her cousin (2:7) to being the queen of Persia. "The king loved Esther more than all the women, and she won grace and favor in his sight more than all the virgins, so that he set the royal crown on her head and made her queen instead of Vashti" (2:17). Winning Miss Persia and all the showbiz fame of the situation could easily go to anyone's head. However, as we read on into chapter 2 and the rest of the book, we discover that it did not go to Esther's head.

There is plenty of illustration in this story of the distasteful sexual power politics of that day. There is plenty of sad evidence in the story too of women merely being treated as sex objects. The question has been asked, Was Esther a heroine or not? For feminist commentators she was not a heroine. She played the role expected of her on her day, and she didn't resist it. Other commentators see that she got her way and influenced the situation in the end by staying involved and so saved her people. She worked in and through a difficult situation in a way that Vashti was not able to do because she opted out. Be that as it may, the story is told in a way that doesn't make any comment of comparison between the two women on this point.

Esther's Predicament

We need to understand the extremely difficult situation that Esther faced (see 2:8, 16). There was an attempt by those surrounding Xerxes to soften the king's sadness and disappointments by indulging his known propensity for beautiful women. A beauty parade was organized for all the eligible young women of the kingdom to be brought to the king's harem, and appallingly they were sent to him one at a time for one night at a time, so he could choose a new queen. "So when the king's order and his edict were proclaimed, and when many young women were gathered in Susa the citadel in the custody of Hegai, Esther also *was taken* into the king's palace" (2:8). She frankly would not have had much choice about it. As her people had been taken into exile, so she was taken into the king's harem. Though it cannot have been at all easy for a well-brought-up Jewess who knew God's Law, the book of Esther is silent about her feelings in the matter. Mordecai was clearly concerned and visited the palace every day (2:11).

Esther's Progress

One thing is especially clear from this story—she was much more than a pretty face! "And the young woman pleased him [Hegai] and won his favor. And he quickly provided her with her cosmetics and her portion of food" (2:9). (Notice the similarities and differences to the story of Daniel [see Daniel 1:8ff.].) A bit further on we are told, "When the turn came for Esther the daughter of Abihail the uncle of Mordecai, who had taken her as his own daughter, to go in to the king, she asked for nothing except what Hegai the king's eunuch, who had charge of the women, advised. Now Esther was winning favor in the eyes of all who saw her" (2:15).

There was much more to Esther than just beauty. There was a humility about her. She could take advice, and she listened with respect also to the advice of Mordecai, her guardian (2:20). As she met with the king, it's clear from the way the story is written that it wasn't just that he was bowled over by her beauty and sexual charm. There was something special about Esther, something about her demeanor and character that was deeply attractive (2:17).

Was she right not to reveal her faith? "Esther had not made known her people or kindred, for Mordecai had commanded her not to make it known" (2:10). We are told this again: "Esther had not made known her kindred or her people," even when she was made queen, "as Mordecai had commanded her, for Esther obeyed Mordecai just as when she was brought up by him" (2:20). Was she right to do so? Again the book of Esther doesn't actually tell us. She was certainly listening to the advice of Mordecai, who may well have been aware of anti-Semitism around them. He was an older and wiser believer whom she loved. But was it really right to keep silent?

I think in many ways there is a subtle piece of advice here. If you are in a dangerous pagan situation, it is probably wise not to flaunt your faith. Please don't misunderstand me, because as we go on in the book of Esther we will discover that at the right time Esther stood up and was counted. When she needed to identify as a believer she stood with her own people, and she was brave and courageous. I am not at all advocating that Christians bury their light under a basket, as Matthew 5:15 puts it; that we hide our Christian profession. But it may be right, in a very hostile situation, not to flaunt our faith. In other words, it is important to build relationships first, to get alongside people, to be seen as a human being, before people understand that we are believers. In other words, it may not be the wisest thing, when you move into your office, to put a fish sign on your computer or to put a text on top of your computer that says, "God loves you. Repent and believe the gospel." It may not be wise, day one, to invite everyone you can find to an evangelistic event. There is surely wisdom here.

Sometimes as Christians we flaunt our faith rather than bravely stand up for it. Maybe the right thing to do in a pagan, hostile environment is to conduct ourselves in such a way that the way we live gets noticed and makes an impression, and to pray for opportunities to speak, and when they come, bravely identify ourselves as believers. That's something for us to think about as we apply the relevance of Esther's behavior to our own situations (cf. Colossians 4:2–6).

Mordecai Takes Responsibility and Is Loyal

In 2:19–23 we see Mordecai sitting at the king's gate. The location described presupposes something of a special, privileged position and implies that he may have been a royal official of some kind. Interestingly enough, this is one way in which the details of the Bible's story are possibly borne out by secular records, as so often proves to be the case. A tablet discovered in 1904 in Persepolis, another royal palace site, contains the name Marduka, a Persian official during the early years of Xerxes' reign. "He served as an accountant on an inspection tour from Susa, and therefore could be the biblical Mordecai, who regularly sat at the king's gate (2:19) like the Persian official mentioned by Herodotus."[5] Karen Jobes's comment is helpful: "Although it may have been too common a name to identify conclusively the Marduka of the Persepolis tablets as the Mordecai in Esther, the correspondence is striking."[6] Mordecai was, it seems, either a minister or someone involved with the doling out of justice because the gate was where you went if you had a dispute and wanted some justice to be done. Certainly Mordecai had become, either through the elevation of his cousin or maybe in his own right, a court official (a civil servant).

A Trailer for Providence

In the last few verses of Esther 2 we begin to get a clue of one of the great themes of the book. In God's good providence, Mordecai learned some information that would be crucial for his good standing with the king later on. He found out about a plot against the king and loyally reported it to Esther, who told the king, which saved his life. The affair was investigated, the culprits were hanged, and the details were recorded "in the book of the chronicles in the presence of the king" (2:23). The Persian kings were generous in rewarding loyalty, so we would expect Mordecai to have been rewarded at that time. However, God's providential timing saw to it that it was remembered later, at a more crucial moment.

Divine Sovereignty and Human Responsibility

Mordecai was in a responsible position, and when he heard something concerning the safety of the king, he handled the information in an honorable and responsible way. He acted as best as he could and as rightly as he knew how, and that proved to be absolutely fundamental later on. Notice what the book of Esther is telling us. Divine sovereignty and human responsibility work together in an inscrutable way. We should also notice that when God's people have problems, God is at work to solve them—ahead of the problems themselves.

The name of God might not be mentioned in the book of Esther, but the activity of God behind the scenes is written on every page. It has rightly been said, "A coincidence is a miracle in which God prefers to remain anonymous."[7] The book of Esther is full of happy coincidences!

One of the great lessons, which we will see in more detail later in the book of Esther, is this: it isn't only when God spectacularly answers prayer—we see a friend healed, or we know God's healing in our own life—and it isn't only when God does something dramatic or miraculous that he is at work. God is wonderfully at work in the little coincidences of our lives, often behind the scenes in an inscrutable way that only time will reveal. Churches that are constantly looking for the miraculous can miss this. We all need to be encouraged to further ponder God's good providence and (as Karen Jobes says) "the miraculous quality of the ordinary."[8]

In the next chapter we will think about how Esther ended up in this strategic position at the time that she did. We will begin to see God's hand in the timing of that too, which can itself be miraculous!

23

The Plot to Destroy the Jews

ESTHER 3—4

WE ENDED CHAPTER 2 with a plot to kill the king being thwarted. In these chapters we read about another plot, this time to destroy the Jews, and Mordecai's and especially Esther's response.

Haman Enters the Scene

At the beginning of Esther 3, "Haman the Agagite, the son of Hammedatha" is introduced to us. The king "advanced him and set his throne above all the officials who were with him" (3:1). That is, he was effectively made the prime minister. Why he was advanced and why he gained the notice of the king we are not told. Nor are we told how long a gap there was between what happened at the end of chapter 2 and the beginning of chapter 3. Mordecai had discovered a plot to kill the king and reported it. At the end of chapter 2 we would have expected Mordecai to be advanced and rewarded for his loyalty and faithfulness. Instead the reader is surprised when chapter 3 opens with the advancement of Haman. As he appears on the scene we soon discover what a thoroughly obnoxious character he is.

It's worth remembering the background timing. The book of Esther opens three years into the reign of Xerxes, with the king's great banquet, and at the end of it Vashti, the queen, refuses to parade her beauty before the drunken party of men. Four years later (seven years into the king's reign), after a disastrous military campaign in Greece, Esther is made the queen. In chapter 3 we are twelve years into the reign of Xerxes (3:7).

When Haman was advanced to the position of prime minister, it would have been common policy and manners to bow before him, as before all senior officials. Mordecai, however, "did not bow down or pay homage" (3:2). Some of the officials, knowing that it was the king who commanded that Haman should be respected, wondered how long Mordecai could get away with this behavior. They weren't prepared to wait too long before they raised the issue and rocked the boat. They said to Mordecai, "'Why do you transgress the king's command?' And when they spoke to him day after day and he would not listen to them, they told Haman, in order to see whether Mordecai's words would stand, for he had told them that he was a Jew" (3:3–4).

"And when Haman saw that Mordecai did not bow down or pay homage to him, Haman was filled with fury" (3:5). His pride was slighted. He was offended by the behavior of Mordecai. But not content to get revenge on Mordecai himself, "he disdained to lay hands on Mordecai alone. So, as they had made known to him the people of Mordecai, Haman sought to destroy all the Jews, the people of Mordecai, throughout the whole kingdom of Ahasuerus" (3:6).

We would hardly believe a character like this in the pages of history were it not for the fact that similar individuals have appeared in our own generation. One only has to think of Hitler's attitude toward the Jews or the behavior of Pol Pot or Stalin in the past century, all of which came on the back of the humanistic optimism at the end of the nineteenth century. The twentieth century saw more genocide, more destruction, and more warfare than any other century in the history of mankind.

Haman, slighted and hurt by the behavior of Mordecai, determined to take revenge and was not content to simply rebuke or exhort Mordecai, but wanted to wipe out the whole Jewish race. What is introduced into the story at this point is nothing less than a pogrom against the Jewish people. This is genocide—the wiping out of the whole people of God. It is an incredibly serious development.

Chapters 1—2 ended with an optimistic view of the future. A Jewish believer had become queen, Mordecai had uncovered a plot against the king, and we would have expected him to be rewarded. Instead, with the kind of twist in circumstances that we often see in our world, Haman was now in a position of great power and planned to wipe out all God's people.

Haman's History

The historical background here is important (see Deuteronomy 25:17–19; 1 Samuel 15). The author is giving us a key clue by calling Haman "the Agagite" (3:1). In 1 Samuel 15 we read that King Saul was told by Samuel, the spokesman for God, to wage war against the Amalekites. He was to wipe them out because of their wickedness. He was to kill the king, Agag. But Saul disobeyed the command of God, sparing the life of Agag. Having won the battle, he also kept the best of the spoils. He tried to hide his greed and offense by saying that the spoil would be offered to God. As a result, God regretted that Saul had been made king and warned him that he would no longer be king; God would raise up somebody else (1 Samuel 15:10, 35ff.).

In Esther 2:5 we are told that Mordecai was a descendant of Kish. In other words, he was from the family of Saul. He would have been aware, from his family history, of the disastrous disobedience of Saul as recorded in 1 Samuel 15. Now Haman, a descendant of Agag, was promoted to be prime minister.

Deuteronomy 25:17–18 tells us about the behavior of the Amalekites and why God was so displeased with them. When God delivered his people out of the land of Israel, the descendants of Esau, the Amalekites, were the first to attack them. They picked off the remnants at the end of the column of the Israelites. When you try to move a large group of people on a walk or a cross-country run, there are always stragglers at the end. The Amalekites attacked the Israelites and picked off the weak and the stragglers—everyone that they could get away with killing.

Deuteronomy 25:18 also tells us the reason they behaved so terribly: they "did not fear God." Their opposition was not just to the people of Israel—their opposition and hostility was to God himself. Bruce Waltke comments, "Amalek represents all the world powers opposed to God's rule."[1] In the telling comment in Exodus 17:16, which describes the Amalekites' attacking the Israelites, God said, "The LORD will have war with Amalek from generation to generation."

In Haman we see a hurt, a dislike, and a hatred that goes beyond seeking revenge on Mordecai to wanting to wipe out all of Mordecai's people. Obviously the Amalekites had not improved with the generations. Here was a real hatred against God and against his people that had continued for generations.

Mordecai's Behavior

What about Mordecai's behavior? Did he not put the whole people of God at risk by his stubborn refusal to pay homage to Haman? We know that the Jews were loyal subjects—they paid homage to other royal officials. So why did Mordecai refuse to pay homage to Haman? Some commentators think Mordecai was just being stubborn and foolish here and that he caused a problem for his people. For example, "In fact, rather than bow, Mordecai risks the fate of all the Jews and puts the whole burden to save them on Esther."[2]

I think it makes more sense to understand that Mordecai believed God's promise. Mordecai as a godly Jew remembered God's covenant promise that he would care for and deliver his people. He remembered the situation from his own family history (1 Samuel 15), and he remembered the comment of the Lord that he would be at war against the Amalekites from generation to generation. Mordecai, whatever the cost, wanted to side with what he knew would be God's reaction to those who were hostile to him and to his people.

Haman's Belief

Haman now sought to destroy the Jews. He first of all cast lots, like our dice (3:7). In other words, he looked to blind chance—we might say he read the horoscope—to determine a propitious time for him to take this action against the Jewish people. With malice he waited from month one (April) to month twelve (March) of the following year (3:7). At least he recognized a sense of something else ordering the affairs of people, but he looked to blind fate and the random casting of lots. As we shall see later, this is in contrast to Esther and Mordecai who looked to the loving providence of a personal God who redeems and cares for his covenant people.

Haman's Appeal

Haman's appeal to the king was clever and manipulative (3:8–10). He asked the king to give him permission to carry out his pogrom. "Then Haman said to King Ahasuerus, 'There is a certain people scattered abroad and dispersed among the peoples in all the provinces of your kingdom'" (3:8a). That was true; there was a particular people—the people of Judah—who were no doubt like other ethnic groups. Secondly, he said, "Their laws are different from those of every other people" (3:8b). That was true too. They were distinctive as God's people, having God's Law and God's revelation. So far he was telling the truth. But notice now how he put his own spin on the facts: "Their laws are different from those of every other people, and they do not keep the king's laws . . ." (3:8b).

We saw at the end of chapter 2 that the people of Judah were law-abiding and loyal to the king. The loyalty of Mordecai in exposing the plot against the king proved that. So Haman's statement was a lie. Because the Jews had their own laws, which were God's laws, Haman implied that they were not keeping the laws of the empire; that simply was not true.

Haman then sought to manipulate the king further by telling him, "It is not to the king's profit to tolerate them" (3:8, or as the NIV translates it, "it is not in the king's best interest"). He appealed to the profit motive and offered the king an extraordinary amount of money—10,000 talents of silver (300 tons), about two-thirds of the king's income from taxes across the whole empire! The king appeared to turn this down (3:11), but Haman's appeal to the king was manipulative, devious, full of half-truths and lies, and subtly sought to justify the genocide of the Jewish people by appearing to have the financial interests of the king at heart.

Haman's behavior was appalling, but if we are honest, we recognize this sort of behavior in our world today too, even in ourselves. Sometimes when we feel hurt about something (be it real or imagined), we have malice and resentment toward others, and this behavior can lead to all kinds of evil and injustice against them. Disputes between individuals can lead whole families to cut off relations with one another for generations. We see a particularly awful example of this in the story of Haman.

The King's Response

What about the behavior of the king? He acquiesced to the desires of Haman, who poignantly is described as "the enemy of the Jews" (3:10), and tells him, "Do with them as it seems good to you" (3:11). Once again it is an extraordinary thing to see a king, the ruler of the superpower of his day, make a decision under pressure on the whim of someone else's opinion. In this case it meant the genocide of a whole people about whom he appeared to care not at all. He is seen here as being far from wise as a king.

The scribes were summoned and an edict written that was sealed with the king's signet ring, which he had given to Haman (3:10). Letters were sent throughout the whole empire by a notable and speedy Persian courier system, an ancient equivalent of the famous Pony Express. The instruction was "to destroy, to kill, and to annihilate all Jews, young and old, women and children, in one day, the thirteenth day of the twelfth month, which is the month of Adar, and to plunder their goods" (3:13).

In light of the plans for the pogrom, we are given a telling description of the king and Haman sitting down to drink together (reminiscent of Herod and Pilate in Luke 23:12). The chapter ends in an understated way: "But the city of Susa was thrown into confusion" (3:15). One can only imagine the consternation and distress that was felt even beyond the people of God themselves.

Esther's Discovery

For Esther the moment of truth had arrived. The question of chapter 4 of the book of Esther is, Will Esther's courage and faith see her through? Will she use her influence for the good of her people?

Esther is the only character in the book with two names—her Hebrew and Persian names (2:7; "Hadassah" means "myrtle" and "Esther" means "star"). It is deeply symbolic of the fact that she was living in two worlds. Would she emerge as a faithful Jew and move away from a past where she was simply controlled by circumstances (with uncomfortable compromises) to make brave and important decisions for the good of her people?

Mordecai learned about Haman's decree and put on sackcloth and ashes, as did many of the Jews (4:1). It appears that the queen was not that well-informed, as apparently she did not yet know about the decree. It seems that in the harem they didn't always get all the news; maybe she was being protected from the media! Furthermore, because of his attire, Mordecai was not allowed beyond the gate into the citadel (4:2). When Esther discovered Mordecai was in sackcloth and ashes, her first reaction was to send him a new set of clothes (4:4) so he could improve his wardrobe and cheer up a bit.

Maybe Esther didn't really want to engage with how serious the situation was. Sometimes that's true of all of us, isn't it? We prefer not to recognize things that may be staring us in the face. We may even disguise inner fears with a shopping trip to cheer us up!

Esther's Choice

The clear choice for Esther, as we shall see, was whether she would put selfish interest—her own—before the well-being of the people of God.

Esther sent her personal attendant, Hathach, to discover why Mordecai was behaving the way he was (4:5). Having explained his conduct, "Mordecai also gave him a copy of the written decree issued in Susa for their destruction, that he might show it to Esther . . ." (4:8a). This was so that she might have a wake-up call and see what was happening. Mordecai explained the situation to her and urged her "to go to the king to beg his favor and plead with him on behalf of her people" (4:8b).

Esther faced the situation with realism (4:10–11). She had reason to feel afraid. She said, "All the king's servants and the people of the king's provinces know that if any man or woman goes to the king inside the inner court without being called, there is but one law—to be put to death, except the one to whom the king holds out the golden scepter so that he may live" (4:11).

We know from artwork from the throne room in Persepolis, one of the palaces of Xerxes, that behind the king stood a soldier with a large axe to protect him and literally hack off the head of anybody who came into the throne room uninvited. So Esther knew she was in danger.

Furthermore, note what she said at the end of verse 11: "But as for me, I have not been called to come in to the king these thirty days." She had not seen her husband for a month—she didn't know whether he was tired of her or whether she would be welcomed. She didn't know if she was any longer the flavor of the month. What Mordecai had asked her would put her in real danger.

We are brought to the heart of the book of Esther in 4:13–16. Notice especially what Mordecai said in reply to Esther's understandable fear.

> "Do not think to yourself that in the king's palace you will escape any more than all the other Jews. For if you keep silent at this time, relief and deliverance will rise for the Jews from another place, but you and your father's house will perish. And who knows whether you have not come to the kingdom for such a time as this?" Then Esther told them to reply to Mordecai, "Go, gather all the Jews to be found in Susa, and hold a fast on my behalf, and do not eat or drink for three days, night or day. I and my young women will also fast as you do. Then I will go to the king, though it is against the law, and if I perish, I perish."

Mordecai told his cousin that she couldn't avoid the issue of choice. She couldn't bury her head and say the situation didn't affect her—because it would. The choice was clear: would she attempt to put self-interest first (which wouldn't work anyway), or would she put the well-being of the people of God first? God cared about the "relief and deliverance" of his people, said Mordecai. Are you encouraged by that as a believer? What God is about— God's number-one agenda—is the relief and deliverance of his people. He loves to bring relief to his followers who are facing severe trials and ultimately plans their deliverance. Why else would God send his dearly beloved Son so that you and I might be delivered and know the relief of being his children, under his care, Heaven having been opened for us? That is God's agenda. That is what God is about. That is the mission statement of God. He is about relief and deliverance. This is what the Bible often calls his saving activity.

To paraphrase what I think is the implication of what Mordecai said: "That is what God is going to do in relation to his people. I not only believe his promise about his being against the Amalekites, but more importantly I believe his promise to relieve and deliver his people. He will not give up on his people, for he delights to show grace and to keep his covenant promises. Relief and deliverance will come as God has promised. If it is not going to come through you (and by the way, Esther, don't think you are indispensable),

God will work it out some other way. But if it is not through you, we will both perish. Esther, there is so much at stake!"

Note carefully how Mordecai's weeping and words echo the words of the prophet in Joel 2:12–13, where God invites his people when in distress to "rend your hearts and not your garments," return to him, and experience his mercy and steadfast love.

There was a lot at stake for the people of God in Esther's day and in the future. The promises of God to Abraham and Moses were at stake. For Ezra and Nehemiah a generation or two later, the restoration of the church in Jerusalem would have been impossible. None of what was then accomplished under God's hand could have happened if God's people had all been wiped out. Ultimately, from where would have come the Christ who was to be born among God's people? The whole future of God's people and his purposes of salvation were at stake.

Mordecai adds crucially in 4:14b, "And who knows whether you have not come to the kingdom for such a time as this?" This is an important verse. Mordecai didn't try to read the hidden hand of providence; he didn't try to second-guess what God would do. Instead he stood on the promises of God—promises of goodness to his people—and encouraged his cousin to act in a way that was right. He said in effect, "Perhaps you are the queen right now, in God's good timing, for the deliverance of his people." Providence can only be seen with clarity, as Mordecai understood, when we look back and see what God has done. Mordecai reminded Esther that her being the queen might be a key moment in God's perfect timing.

Providence and Responsibility

It is important for us to notice that the day the genocide of the people of Judah was announced to take place was the very day before the celebration of the Passover (3:12ff.; Exodus 12:2, 6).[3] God had delivered them out of Egypt in the great redemptive act of the Old Testament, which the Jews celebrated every year in the Feast of Passover. Now would God deliver them again? Would he deliver them again from the Amalekites as he had promised (Exodus 17:8–16)? Mordecai saw that this could be God's perfect timing, that Esther was the queen in a pagan empire for such a time as this. Although Mordecai trusted in God's sovereign providence to bring relief and deliverance to his people, he reminded Esther of her responsibility in the matter. The Bible teaches on the one hand the sovereignty of God that works itself out in the providential care of his people, and on the other hand our responsibility as God's people to act rightly and wisely in challenging and difficult situations. The strategic placing of believers in key posts to influence the course of events "for such a time as this" (4:14) is surely evidence of God's sovereign providence.

In the previous chapter I said that the book of Esther doesn't mention prayer. It isn't mentioned specifically, but it is strongly implied here in 4:16. Karen Jobes helpfully comments, "Prayer is usually assumed to accompany fasting in biblical idiom."[4] The Jews normally fasted for only a day, but Esther called for a three-day fast. Moving from just passively listening to what Mordecai said to her, she now began to call the shots. She had made her decision. She decided not to put self-interest before the well-being of God's people.

God's honor is wrapped up in the care and love of his people. It's no accident that in the New Testament the church is called the Body of Christ. That's how Jesus feels about those whom he has loved and redeemed. Esther made the decision to identify with God's people however costly that would be for her. Esther needed to be reminded to go with the flow of God's plan or to risk being bypassed by God. She made the right choice.

This passage reminds us of something of crucial importance: God's agenda is the relief and deliverance of his people. That is always his agenda. God always wants to save people, to show them his grace and love and bring them to Heaven. In the church, because of self-interest and protection of our comfort zones, we sometimes fail to follow God's missionary heart to win a new generation for Christ. If we don't want the church to do anything other than that which brings us personal comfort, and we therefore stand in the way of God's purpose to redeem a new generation, we will find ourselves going against the flow of God's plan and will simply be bypassed by God. That is a very serious comment. In the years that I have been a Christian minister, I have seen this happen in churches. I have seen senior Christian leaders who have not gone with the flow of God's agenda, the missionary heart of God to bring relief and deliverance to his people. They have turned in on themselves, allowed the church to become self-absorbed, pandered to personal agendas, and failed to obey the missionary call of God to save the lost and to be a light to the world. It has been well said by Archbishop William Temple, "The Church is the only organization that does not exist for itself but for those who live outside of it." It exists supremely for the glory of God, and he is glorified when we follow his agenda and are the people he wants us to be. When we refuse to obey him, God raises up other people who will. His plan will be fulfilled, but we will miss out on the blessing he meant for us.

Mordecai told Esther, "If you keep silent at this time, relief and deliverance will rise for the Jews from another place" (4:14). The issue for Esther and us is, Will we put our own personal comfort first or will we seek to honor

God and his purposes by caring for his people? We do well to ask ourselves the question, Is the well-being of God's people high on my agenda? or Do I see the church existing for me? The challenge of this passage is to put the well-being of God's people before our own.

When I was a minister in Harold Wood (London), I remember talking to our organist, a fine Christian man. Thanking him for his music ministry, I said to him, "You are a classically trained musician, so some of the things you play for the congregation might not be what you really like playing." He replied, "That's true, but what I like in terms of the music of the church is not important—the well-being of the whole congregation is what matters. I am here to serve the glory of God and the well-being of his people." Oh, for more Christian servants like that!

When we have a choice in the office or in our neighborhood to nail our colors to the mast and identify ourselves with the people of God—to stand up and identify with them as believers whatever the cost—what decision will we make? Gordon McConville's comment is helpful: "Taking the side of right (specifically standing up for God's people) will involve personal risk."[5] For many Christians in the world today, owning the name of Christ brings personal danger and suffering. By comparison, we in the West have largely not yet had to count the cost in that way, though the increasing marginalization of our Christian faith is bringing growing problems. In the UK we have seen a number of cases that threaten the freedom of Christians to express Christian values.

Will we rise to the challenge like Esther did, seeking the glory of God, the agenda of God, and the good of God's people much more than our own personal safety and comfort? Will we know as a result the joyful blessing of God because of that obedience, or will we simply get bypassed?

In the next chapter we will see how God brought that deliverance about.

24

The Reversal of "Fortune" Begins

ESTHER 5—7

CHAPTER 4 ENDS WITH Esther saying, "I will go to the king, though it is against the law, and if I perish, I perish" (4:16). She decided to do the right thing, whatever the personal cost, and left the outcome in God's hands.

Chapter 5 rushes on to tell us what began to happen that would lead to a complete reversal of the whole difficult situation that has been described so far in the book. Haman on the one hand had been promoted to prime minister and plotted evil against the Jews, but Mordecai had been forgotten even though he had reported an assassination plot against the king.

Esther 5—7 describes a reversal of fortune for these two men: Haman is brought down, and Mordecai is exalted.

Responsibility in Action

Throughout the book of Esther we see the sovereignty of God, but also how he works through the obedience of his people.

Esther's Courage

Esther went to the king immediately after a period of fasting (4:16; 5:1). Her asking for a fast for three days shows how seriously she viewed the situation. The young women who were with her fasted also, as well as all the Jews in Susa (4:16). In Jewish thinking this implied that they were both praying and fasting.

Without delay, after this period of prayer, Esther "put on her royal robes" (literally the Hebrew reads, "put on royalty") on the third day and went to see her husband as his queen (5:1). She "stood in the inner court of the king's palace, in front of the king's quarters, while the king was sitting on his royal throne inside the throne room opposite to the entrance to the palace" (5:1). This was a highly dangerous situation because nobody was allowed to go into the king's presence without being summoned by him; they could not go in uninvited. Unless he held up his scepter to them, they would be killed. Esther went into this dangerous and difficult situation without knowing what the outcome would be. But she only went in after prayer and fasting. That is a great lesson for us.

In the challenges of life, our supreme example is the Lord Jesus himself, who before every major period of ministry, as recorded in the Gospels, had a time of prayer (e.g., Mark 1:35). Before this major challenge of her life Esther prayed fervently and seriously. This is a lesson we as Christians would do well to learn. Only prayer will see us through. As a well-known hymn puts it:

Stand up, stand up for Jesus,
Stand in his strength alone;
The arm of flesh will fail you,
Ye dare not trust your own.
Put on the gospel armor,
Each piece put on *with prayer;*
Where duty calls, or danger,
Be never wanting there.

—*George Duffield*[1]

One of the problems of the church in the West today is that we think we can win the battle for Christ by our own cleverness, communication skills, or new and innovative programs. However helpful these may be, we will never win the spiritual battle unless we pray. When we pray we show our utter dependence upon God.

In England, many local, district, and county councils have prayers to begin their meetings. In the area where I worked, Lewes District Council decided to modernize their procedures. They decided to abandon prayers before council meetings, abandon the appointment of a chaplain, and abandon the holding of a yearly civic church service. They were in danger of throwing out the baby with the bathwater. I raised my concerns with the leader of the district council and explained, "If you abandon prayer, you are saying as a group of councilors that you can do your job in your own strength. You have some hard decisions to make, and surely you need God's help." He was shocked and said, "Do you really think it is as bad as that?" To which I replied, "Yes, I do. If we become prayerless, we become dependent on ourselves alone, and that is just human pride." Sadly, though embarrassed, the council did not relent. However, at the same time the county council, which was a more important body, introduced prayers and asked me to lead them, a step in the right direction.

Esther knew acutely the danger and difficulty of the situation she faced in a pagan world. She was in a perilous situation. Even her position as queen was precarious. Esther 4 left us with the impression that she had become queen for a reason and that if she was obedient to God, she would be successful. Nonetheless, Esther, by her appeal for the support and prayer of the Jewish community in Susa, understood that unless God was in this, unless God helped her, her endeavors would fail.

We need to understand this principle much more in the church today. Why is the prayer meeting so often the least attended meeting in the life of the church? Though people may be praying in other ways in home Bible study groups and so on, we do need to be sure that the church is praying seriously as the church. Since prayer is such a privilege and is a crucial weapon in our warfare, why do we not make it more of a priority? If we are to break through in a pagan world or to be successful against huge human odds, we need to be like Esther—we need to be people of prayer.

"And when the king saw Queen Esther standing in the court, she won favor in his sight, and he held out to Esther the golden scepter that was in his hand" (5:2). When she appeared, the king's heart melted. We would do well to remember that this man could be barbarous. We know from Herodotus (*The Histories*) that on one occasion, when invading Greece, engineers could not finish building a bridge because of storms, so it was only completed after a delay. Xerxes had all the engineers executed in spite of their best efforts. When Xerxes got mad, he could be mad indeed! But he also really loved Esther. He was glad to see her, was open to her requests, and was even generous in his response (though 5:3, 6 and 7:2 were not meant to be taken literally). "And the king said to her, 'What is it, Queen Esther? What is your request? It shall be given you, even to the half of my kingdom'" (5:3).

Esther's Wisdom

Esther was tactful and invited the king and Haman to a feast. We have already discovered that the king liked feasts—he loved a dinner party (she knew her husband well, didn't she?). One of the great structural features of the book of Esther is banquets. There are two feasts at the beginning of the book (1:3; 2:18), two feasts here (5:4; 7:2), and two feast days at the end of the book (8:17; 9:22). The king was glad that the queen wanted to hold a dinner party for him and the prime minister, and he was eager to get on with it. "Then the king said, 'Bring Haman quickly, so that we may do as Esther has asked'" (5:5). At the conclusion of the first dinner party, which was successful and went off without incident, the king was still wondering what Esther's request was (5:6). He was no doubt intrigued and couldn't believe his good fortune— he was going to have special fare yet again with the woman he most loved (5:7). Esther knew how to get her husband's favor. She knew that the way to a man's heart is through his stomach, as an old saying goes. So she set out to wine and dine him again.

Haman's Self-Absorption

Haman was absolutely delighted to be included. "And Haman went out that day joyful and glad of heart" (5:9). But his euphoria soon turned to anger on his journey home when Mordecai did not bow down before him. We get insight into Haman's character and self-absorption when he managed to restrain his anger in order to go home and boast about himself to all his family and friends (5:10–12). "And Haman recounted to them the splendor of his riches, the number of his sons, all the promotions with which the king had honored him, and how he had advanced him above the officials and the servants of the king. Then Haman said, 'Even Queen Esther let no one but me come with the king to the feast she prepared. And tomorrow also I am invited by her together with the king'" (5:11–12). He was euphoric about how well he was doing. He was absorbed with his own importance, just like a lot of people in our modern world. The book of Proverbs tells us aptly that "pride goes before destruction" (16:18). We as the readers of the story are beginning to realize what is going to happen, but Haman was oblivious to it all.

Even in the midst of self-delusion and self-flattery the desire for revenge was still eating away at Haman's heart. Mordecai was a thorn in his side, and egged on by his wife and friends, he felt good at the thought of eradicating this difficult Jew on a gallows seventy-five feet high (5:14).

Esther's Responsible Action

In contrast to Haman, Esther saw the pressing need to act *responsibly*. The sovereignty of God working through the events of history for the good of his people does not absolve us from our responsibility to God. It rather calls us to be obedient to him. Responsibility before God demands two things. It demands courage on the one hand and wisdom on the other. Not only did Esther bravely lay aside her own personal interests and put the interests of her people first, she was also wise in the way she sought the king's favor. She handled the situation with wisdom and tact.

As Christians in a pagan world we need courage, but not the kind of naive, foolhardy courage that sometimes substitutes sheer folly for bravery. We need to consider a course of action, take action that is thoughtful, pray it through, and match it with courage. Esther was willing to put herself on the line and was willing to risk her own head. We see exemplified in Esther the lovely combination of courage and wisdom that the Bible commends for God's people. Her conviction of what was the right thing to do galvanized her into prayerful action, and from this point on in the story she becomes the dominant player.

The man who led me to Christ, David Lewis, told me about a neighbor who was hostile to the gospel and how impossible it was to have a conversation with him about the Lord. One day he noticed a sailing dinghy in his neighbor's back garden and asked him if he liked to sail. He said that he loved sailing and asked David if he liked sailing. David bravely said yes and was then asked to go sailing with his neighbor, to "crew" for him. As David had never done this, he checked out every book in the library on sailing and then went sailing with his neighbor. They had a wonderful time, and barriers were broken down. On the second time out sailing, he explained the gospel to his neighbor and led him to Christ! He had taken the time and the trouble to get on his neighbor's wavelength and show brave wisdom in getting a hearing for what he knew God wanted him to communicate. Though in very different circumstances, Esther showed brave wisdom in getting prayerfully on her husband's wavelength in order to be obedient to what God wanted her to do to further his kingdom.

One worry, however, remains at the end of Esther 5. In the light of Haman's determination to get Mordecai hanged (5:14), has Esther acted too late to save her cousin's life?

The "Coincidences" of Providence

As we continue to work our way through the book of Esther, we see again and again the truly amazing ways that God works out his will on behalf of his people.

Sleepless in Susa

The whole book of Esther turns on chapter 6, which describes a sleepless night. Why was the king sleepless in Susa? Did he eat too much at the feast or drink too much? Was he so overcome by the beauty of the queen that he couldn't wait to see her the following night and discover her wish and request? We do not know, but had that not happened in God's good providence, he would not have had "the chronicles," the history of brave and memorable deeds, read to him to help him go to sleep (6:1). Some lowly servant was awakened in order to read the chronicles to the king who couldn't sleep. We are beginning to see comic irony displayed in the way the book of Esther was written. We see God at work behind the scenes. Even the sleepless night of the king was crucial in the reversal of the fortune of God's people.

The King's Early Morning Resolve

Fortuitously, one of the passages read to the king that night told how Mordecai had saved his life. He then asked, "What honor or distinction has been bestowed on Mordecai for this?" (6:3). Persian kings were generous in rewarding loyalty, but in this case he discovered that Mordecai had been forgotten and remained unrewarded. Just as he was wondering what to do and who to ask for advice, Haman came in early to work—another "coincidence." It is interesting to notice once again that Xerxes seemed unable to do anything, despite all his power as the king, without asking somebody else what to do. Somebody told him that the prime minister had just happened to arrive in the outer court, and he requested that Haman be brought in.

Illusions of Grandeur

Once again, with incredible, comic irony, the king said to Haman, "What should be done to the man whom the king delights to honor?" and Haman said to himself, "Whom would the king delight to honor more than me?" (6:6). Haman was oblivious to the reality of the situation. Then Haman dreamt up a picture of how he could be honored. The deluded Haman said, "For the man whom the king delights to honor, let royal robes be brought, which the king has worn, and the horse that the king has ridden, and on whose head a royal crown is set . . . and let them lead him on the horse through the square of the city, proclaiming before him: 'Thus shall it be done to the man whom the king delights to honor'" (6:7–9). We know from historical records of the time that the Persians put a crown on the head of some of their royal horses. Haman was asking to be dressed like the king and to ride the horse of the king. He was almost asking to be treated like the king himself. "Then the king said to Haman, 'Hurry; take the robes and the horse, as you have said, and do so to Mordecai the Jew, who sits at the king's gate. Leave out nothing that you have mentioned" (6:10). Haman was absolutely shocked! He was going to have to put into operation his own suggestions, not for himself but for his hated enemy!

As we read the story we cannot help but chuckle to ourselves and praise God for his amazing sovereignty in human events.

A loyal deed by Mordecai was remembered in the nick of time, in fact, at the best time. We had ended chapter 2 disappointed that Mordecai had not been honored, but in God's providential timing this came at exactly the right time.

Have you ever noticed, looking back, how God's perfect, providential care of his people is often, it seems, last-minute, so that his people will trust him? That is a remarkable and merciful thing. I remember as a young Christian learning to pray to God about certain situations. I began to spot what I thought initially were coincidences. Then I began to understand that they weren't co-incidences at all; there were too many of them to be put down as that. Rather, I recognized the hand of God. That is what we are seeing here in Esther 6.

When I was a vicar in Harold Wood, London, we had a real concern about doing some youth work with unchurched teenagers who walked through the parish every day to a local school. We wanted to open a drop-in center and offer youth an "Introducing Jesus" course as soon as we could. Just a few yards away was a hall owned by the local council, which was the second most financially needy council in the United Kingdom. They decided to sell the hall and were asking one million pounds for it. We didn't have the resources to buy it but felt it was ideal for our purposes. So as a church we began to pray. On behalf of our elders I went with an accountant and a youth worker to see the leader of the council.

We talked about the youth problems in the area—truancy and drugs—and I told him that we really wanted to do work with young people but needed a facility to do it. The church would pay for a full-time youth worker to be based in the hall, and I asked him if the council would meet us halfway and give us the hall for a nominal rent. He said, "We can't do that." I reminded him that without some serious youth work, much more would need to be spent on the drug and truancy problems in the future. He said, "We need to sell the property."

However, the opposition parties in the council supported the idea of the hall being used as a community center for youth. The ruling party, who prided themselves in being the party that cared, felt obliged in the end to take our suggestion seriously. Wonderfully, the outcome was that we did in fact open a new center in the hall, which was leased to us for twenty years for one pound per year.

The sequel to the story is even more amazing. Here we began to see God's providence at work. If God's people take just a little step out in faith, however tentatively, they find that God is there at work already. We needed the parking lot at the side of the hall because large numbers of people were coming to church. I went back to the leader of the council and asked for half of the parking lot—we didn't need it all. Having given me the hall for one pound per year, he said, "Don't push your luck, vicar! We are going to build some houses on that lot." Beyond our hopes and dreams, when they did excavations in the parking lot, they discovered it had main water pipes running underneath, and they weren't allowed to build on half of it. So we got the half of the parking lot we needed as well!

I have told you this story as an example of the sovereignty of God and his providential care. The superintendency of God even came down to the detail of the water mains having been laid down thirty-five years earlier so that his people could have the facilities they needed to do what he wanted them to do in the first place. The "coincidences" of providence—God's perfect, last-minute, faith-provoking timing—were then and still are an enormous encouragement to his church.

Reversals I

One of the other great themes of the book of Esther is the reversal of humanly impossible situations. There are two reversals in chapters 6 and 7. First of all, in chapter 6 Mordecai was honored. Haman had to personally parade Mordecai, whom he despised, through the streets, fulfilling for him the honor he had wanted for himself. How very embarrassing and humiliating for Haman, but how wonderful for the forgotten Mordecai! Haman then had a warning from his wife and friends, who by the way, had earlier told him to build a seventy-five-foot-high gallows in anticipation of getting the king's approval to hang Mordecai (5:14). But now "Haman told his wife Zeresh and all his friends everything that had happened to him. Then his wise men and his wife Zeresh said to him, 'If Mordecai, before whom you have begun to fall, is of the Jewish people, you will not overcome him but will surely fall before him'" (6:13). His wife had enough sense to understand what was going on and indeed what God was doing to protect his people.

In Esther 6, God prevented evil plans from being successful, and Haman for all his personal pride was defeated and humiliated. "Mordecai returned to the king's gate. But Haman hurried to his house, mourning and with his head covered" (6:12). He was devastated.

We would do well to recall Haman's previous attitude toward Mordecai. Even at the moment of his greatest boasting, as recorded in Esther 5, he said that all his possessions and achievements were "worth nothing to me, so long as I see Mordecai the Jew sitting at the king's gate" (5:13). Haman had gained success and fortune, great possessions and status, and yet it did not satisfy him.

He was the typical pagan. Here was a person who had done well in business, had come to the top of the pile, and was possessed by his own importance. He had a heart that was not open to God and therefore a heart dissatisfied with what he had. He held a festering resentment against Mordecai, and this resentment led to bitterness of heart, which was obsessed with his own position and possessions and was closed to the things of God.

However, Haman's personal revenge was thwarted, and an amazing reversal happened. God had turned everything upside down. The humanly impossible happened. At just the right time, Mordecai was honored rather than hanged.

While Haman was in torment about what had just happened, he had no time to catch his breath before the king's eunuchs came to collect him for the queen's second dinner party (6:14). Life doesn't stop in the midst of dilemmas.

Reversals II

The second reversal is seen in chapter 7. Esther didn't reveal her request until the second dinner party. Remember, the king had said in effect, "Whatever you want, Esther, I will give it to you—even half of my kingdom" (5:3; 7:2). That probably was a customary way of speaking; he probably didn't mean it literally. It was a way of saying, "I'm in a good mood, and I will give you as much as I can."

Esther's Ploy

Esther picked the right moment at the second feast to make her request. We may wonder why she waited until then to do it. It would appear that she was using her feminine charm to string her husband along. She wanted to ensure that she had him in the best possible frame of mind. Probably by the second dinner party, the last person Xerxes wanted to be present was Haman. Cleverly, Esther had engineered a situation where the king wanted time with his beautiful wife and the wretched prime minister was still there! Esther had set it up in such a way that the king was perhaps beginning to resent the prime minister, but Haman's presence was crucial as Esther presented her request.

Esther's Request

Up until now Esther had not revealed that she was a Jew, but she now revealed her identity and her request.

If I have found favor in your sight, O king, and if it please the king, let my
life be granted me for my wish, and my people for my request. For we have
been sold [a cunning reference to the fact that money was offered to the
king for the decree of annihilation], I and my people, to be destroyed, to be
killed, and to be annihilated. If we had been sold merely as slaves, men and
women, I would have been silent, for our affliction is not to be compared
with the loss to the king. (7:3–4)

Then Xerxes said to Queen Esther, "Who is he, and where is he, who has dared
to do this?" (7:5). This is where the dinner party became tense. Esther said,
"A foe and enemy! This wicked Haman!" (7:6). She was bravely turning the
tables, saying in effect, "The person who is your prime minister is not just an
enemy of mine—he is an enemy of yours and the state." "Then Haman was
terrified before the king and the queen" (7:6). Haman had not until this time
known Esther's identity as a Jew (she had followed Mordecai's advice and
kept her identity hidden).

Just when we think things are at an all-time low for Haman, he manages
to make things even worse. The king was so cross that he left the room and
went into the garden for a walk to cool down and clear his head. He was filled
with rage and was wondering what he should do about what he had heard.
Haman remained to plead with Esther for his life. Haman "saw that harm was
determined against him by the king. And the king returned from the palace
garden to the place where they were drinking wine, as Haman was falling on
the couch where Esther was. And the king said, 'Will he even assault the queen
in my presence, in my own house?'" (7:7–8).

Haman had made matters even worse. He didn't think he could further
appeal to the king, so he appealed to the queen instead. This was a breach of
palace protocol, for it was not permitted for him to remain with the queen on
his own. Nevertheless, he appealed to the queen and fell down "on the couch"
where she was reclining. Esther was no doubt pleased and relieved about how
things were going and was waiting for the saga to unfold. The king walked in
at just the wrong yet providential moment and thought Haman was assaulting
the queen, which made him even more angry. If there was any doubt at all in
his mind who to get rid of—the queen or the prime minister—the issue was
now settled.

Haman Exposed

Haman's plot was now fully exposed, and he was seen to be the enemy of
the king and his best interests. The palace staff acted quickly: "As the word
left the mouth of the king, they covered Haman's face" (7:8). It seems that

Haman wasn't all that popular with the staff, for Harbona, one of the eunuchs, reminded the king that Haman had prepared a gallows on which to hang Mordecai, who had saved the king's life (7:9). Perhaps the king began to wonder, since Haman wanted to get rid of the man who had saved his life, whether he too was implicated in a plot against him. Harbona gave the king the information about the gallows standing at Haman's house, and now the king connected the dots and was more decisive than usual. "And the king said, 'Hang him on that.' So they hanged Haman on the gallows that he had prepared for Mordecai. Then the wrath of the king abated" (7:9b–10). The gallows was probably a huge stake on which the person was hanged or impaled. To coin a phrase, Haman was hoisted by his own petard. He was hanged on the gallows that was meant for Mordecai.

This then was the second reversal. Not only was Mordecai honored rather than hanged, Haman was hanged on the gallows outside his own house, the gallows intended for Mordecai.

Application

It is worth reminding ourselves at the end of these chapters of three important things.

First of all, *God loves to rule and overrule the humanly inevitable.* The things that we consider so difficult, so impossible, so humanly unresolvable, God loves to overrule and work through, for his glory and for the good of his people. The ultimate reversal (the technical term for such a situation is *peripety*) is the cross. On Good Friday the message seemed to be that Jesus was defeated, but Easter Sunday revealed the full message: Jesus defeated Satan and won salvation for his people (Acts 2:23–24). How truly wonderful and glorious that is!

The well-known story is told of how the news of Wellington's defeat of Napoleon at the Battle of Waterloo came through slowly by semaphore across the channel to England. The message read "Wellington defeated," and a nation's heart sank. But then the full message came through: "Wellington defeated Napoleon," and what joy that brought!

Secondly, *God's people should never despair or be pessimistic in the affairs of life, but keep trusting and remaining dependent upon God.* This passage, as does all of God's Word, calls us to be confident in the sovereignty of our God, to be confident in the fact that our God reigns. Even if we can't always see his purposes or understand his ways, we need to trust him to act for the well-being of his people, whom he will ultimately save. The Psalms are full of encouragement to trust God in the ups and down of life, assuring us that his steadfast covenant love will see us through (a favorite of mine is Psalm 62). The New Testament puts all of this into an eternal dimension. God will save, keep, bless, and bring his people to Heaven, and no one will prevent him from doing that. We can be confident in the sovereignty of God and his providential care.

I like the way Paul Williams puts it:

> God delights in turning around apparently "impossible" situations. He loves to act when everything seems lost with no apparent way to change circumstances. It is then that God is glorified as the unmistakable architect of events. Knowing that should give us the determination to keep plodding away at building the kingdom of God, even when (and especially when) everything seems lost.[2]

In the light of who Jesus is and his victorious death and resurrection, it is unthinkable that the Lord will fail the people that he came to save, in life or in death. Confidence in Christ's ability to save, keep, and help along the pathway to Heaven is patent in the apostolic teaching of the New Testament. The Lord, to whom all authority has been given, can be completely trusted. Paul wrote, "It is no longer I who live, but Christ who lives in me. And the life I now live in the flesh I live by faith in the Son of God, who loved me and gave himself for me" (Galatians 2:20). Peter added,

> Blessed be the God and Father of our Lord Jesus Christ! According to his great mercy, he has caused us to be born again to a living hope through the resurrection of Jesus Christ from the dead, to an inheritance that is imperishable, undefiled, and unfading, kept in heaven for you, who by God's power are being guarded through faith for a salvation ready to be revealed in the last time. (1 Peter 1:3–5)

Third, *we need to remember Esther's reaction. She acted responsibly, under God's hand and in obedience to what was known of his will for his people.* We have seen the same pattern in the lives of Ezra and Nehemiah.

May we too trust God's sovereign power, and in the difficult decisions of life may we responsibly pray and act under his hand, in obedience to his known will. Thus may God have the praise and God's people the blessing!

As Paul encouraged us in Colossians, "Continue steadfastly in prayer, being watchful in it with thanksgiving. . . . Walk in wisdom toward outsiders, making the best use of the time" (Colossians 4:2, 5).

25

Deliverance for the Jews

ESTHER 8—9

AS THE STORY CONTINUES, we see Esther's courage taking further action for God's glory and the deliverance of her people.

Speaking Up in God's Good Time

Chapter 8 begins with Esther and Mordecai safe. "On that day King Ahasuerus gave to Esther the house [the estate] of Haman, the enemy of the Jews. And Mordecai came before the king, for Esther had told what he was to her" (8:1). In other words, Esther revealed not only her relationship to Mordecai but how much he meant to her. "And the king took off his signet ring, which he had taken from Haman, and gave it to Mordecai [Mordecai was now effectively the prime minister] and Esther set Mordecai over the house of Haman" (8:2). That which the king had given to her, she gave to Mordecai to look after.

Despite all the possibilities of what might have taken place, Esther and Mordecai were now secure. We move from the amazing events of the last chapter, where Haman met a tragic end and his just deserts, into something that is deadly serious. Despite the security for Esther and Mordecai, God's people still faced annihilation because the decree of Haman still stood. Haman had been hanged, but the future of the people of God still hung in the balance.

Esther's Choice

Esther was facing a major choice. She was now personally secure, but would she be sidetracked by her own interests or would she put her life on the line for her people? We discover that Esther was forthright in a good cause, God's cause. She was brave and selfless. "Then Esther spoke again to the king" (8:3).

Remember that every time she did this was a life-threatening situation for her. Unless the king held up his scepter, she would be executed. "She fell at his feet and wept and pleaded with him to avert the evil plan of Haman the Agagite and the plot he had devised against the Jews" (8:3–4).

It seems that Xerxes (Ahasuerus), once his beloved queen was secure and his new hero and first minister Mordecai was in a position of security and power, wasn't too worried about what would happen to the rest of the Jews. Esther, with tremendous bravery and selflessness, put her life on the line again. When the king held out the golden scepter to Esther, she diplomatically summed up her concerns: "If it please the king, and if I have found favor in his sight, and if the thing seems right before the king, and I am pleasing in his eyes, let an order be written to revoke the letters devised by Haman the Agagite, the son of Hammedatha, which he wrote to destroy the Jews who are in all the provinces of the king. For how can I bear to see the calamity that is coming to my people? Or how can I bear to see the destruction of my kindred?" (8:5–6). This last moving phrase is graphically translated by the NIV: "How can I bear to see the destruction of my family?"

Esther's Concern

Esther's concern was about her kith and kin, her race and her nation. In terms of the old covenant, her concern was about the people of God—not just about her own well-being but about the well-being of the church of her day. She put herself on the line, and her own interests and security were put aside because of an overriding concern for the well-being of the people of God, who were facing annihilation. We would do well to note the top priority concern of Esther's heart.

She spoke up bravely, courageously, and forthrightly in the good cause of the safety of God's people. But notice that even as we admire Esther's bravery and the clarity of her priorities, the story also hints that she was no saint. As we shall see as the story develops, Esther wasn't perfect, and neither was Mordecai. Indeed, we are reminded of the list of Old Testament heroes of faith in Hebrews 11 who were all flawed in one way or another.

Esther's Request

The queen asked the king to reverse the edict of Haman (8:5). The problem stated by the king was that since the laws of the Medes and Persians could not be revoked, Haman's decree could not be undone. But the king offered a way out and washed his hands of the problem at the same time: "But you [plural] may write as you please with regard to the Jews, in the name of the king, and seal it with the king's ring, for an edict written in the name of the king and sealed with the king's ring cannot be revoked" (8:8). Xerxes was saying to the queen, "You and Mordecai find a way out of this—I cannot lose face," and that was precisely what they did (with his authority). Mordecai cleverly worked with the king's scribes to write a new edict that would be sealed by the king, declaring that on the day that Haman had decreed for the Jewish people to be attacked and annihilated, the king would allow the Jews in every city to gather and defend themselves, "to destroy, to kill, and to annihilate any armed force of any people or province that might attack them, children and women included, and to plunder their goods" (8:11). Although scholars debate the meaning of "children and women included," it probably refers to the Jewish women and children who were being attacked rather than the Jews being given the right to attack their enemies' women and children (see NIV translation of 8:11). "The king's edict granted the Jews in every city the right to assemble and protect themselves; to destroy, kill and annihilate the armed men of any nationality or province who might attack them and their women and children, and to plunder the property of their enemies."[1] This defense was allowed "on one day throughout all the provinces of King Ahasuerus, on the thirteenth day of the twelfth month, which is the month of Adar" (8:12).

This new decree then, which was issued and sent around swiftly by the king's Pony Express (8:14), said that the Jewish people could defend themselves, the emphasis being not on unprovoked attack but on their ability to defend themselves and to do all that was necessary for their safety and security. However, the author of the book of Esther is careful to tell us three times that when they defended themselves and defeated their enemies, they did not repeat the sin of Saul in dealing with the Amalekites—they took no plunder (9:10, 15–16). In this respect, at least, they acted with restraint.

Joy for the Jews

The Jews felt an incalculable relief and joy that they were not going to be annihilated and that they could defend themselves. As a result of the decree, "the Jews had light and gladness and joy and honor" (8:16). They had "light"—brightness of spirit like we feel at the dawn of a beautiful new day—as well as a new, joyful appreciation of God's goodness to them and a new standing and respect in the community. Wouldn't it be a wonderful thing to say of all Christian people and of the church in our time that the Lord's people "had light and gladness and joy and honor"? After Haman's decree it looked as if the Jews would have darkness and sorrow and misery and extinction. But

God turned it around so that his people had great hope of deliverance. This signaled the coming tremendous reversal. Receiving the edict brought such joy and gladness that the Jews celebrated with "a feast and a holiday" (8:17). Furthermore this reversal affected all the Jews in the empire, including those who had returned to Jerusalem and Judea. Esther, under God's mighty hand, was the means of the deliverance not only of the Jews in Susa but throughout the land.

Fear for Their Enemies

Notice what else we are told: "And in every province and in every city, wherever the king's command and his edict reached, there was gladness and joy among the Jews, a feast and a holiday. And many from the peoples of the country declared themselves Jews, for fear of the Jews had fallen on them" (8:17; cf. 9:2). Evidently some people became Jewish proselytes, as Rahab had at Jericho. Others perhaps pretended to be Jews because they were fearful of the new power and standing of the people of God. A new fear came upon the pagan nations, and there was great respect for God's people.

In 9:3 we also read, "All the officials of the provinces and the satraps and the governors and the royal agents also helped the Jews, for the fear of Mordecai had fallen on them." In 8:15 we were told that "Mordecai went out from the presence of the king in royal robes of blue and white, with a great golden crown and a robe of fine linen and purple, and the city of Susa shouted and rejoiced." Mordecai, in other words, was popular and deeply respected and grew in power and influence as prime minister (9:4).

I am reminded of what happened to followers of Jesus when Emperor Constantine became a Christian in the fourth century. Suddenly the despised minority of Christians became the key religious grouping of the empire, were held in awe, and became in a way the established faith of the Roman Empire. In contrast, every institution in our society in the West today has been under attack, even the Christian church. Bible-believing Christians are marginalized and are maligned in unprecedented ways. Persecution worldwide is increasing alarmingly, and our right to stand up for our faith and freely witness about our Lord is being challenged in many ways, even in the once-Christian West.

An Allusion to God?

Regarding the phrase "the fear of Mordecai had fallen on them" (9:3), scholars point out that it evokes a phrase found earlier in Genesis 31:42, describing Isaac's witness ("the fear of Isaac," KJV), meaning that the fear of Isaac's God fell upon them. This is another way of saying that the fear of God fell upon the people in Mordecai's day. I agree with Gordon McConville that the phrase "the fear of Mordecai" is "one of the most suggestive allusions to God in the book," meaning "The fear of God fell upon them."[2]

We need this in our own generation. I hope you long for it. I hope you love your country and long for the fear of God to fall again upon your nation more than anything else. The British were once described as "people of the Book." Sadly, that is no longer the case. I hope you long for a day when God's Word is again loved and honored in your nation, when the Christian faith is respected and followed. What a contrast that would be compared to the huge erosion of the Christian faith and its values we have witnessed in our generation. I hope you pray and long for a reversal in the fortune of the church of our day in the West (though elsewhere it is thriving!).

The book of Esther asks us, How much do we care about that? How much do we look for a reversal, under God's hand, in the fortunes of the church in our day? How much do we long for more people to come to experience the joy of knowing Christ and the forgiveness of sins, to discover the reason for which they were made, to not be hopeless and without God in the world but rather to know a relationship with the living God through his Son and to have the sure hope of eternal life? How much do you long for a healthy and lively church for your grandchildren where they will hear the great truths of the gospel? The book of Esther urges us to ask questions about the survival of our identity as the people of God throughout every generation.

Reversal III

In Esther 9 the key reversal, by God's good providence, comes about. "Now in the twelfth month, which is the month of Adar, on the thirteenth day of the same, when the king's command and edict were about to be carried out, on the very day when the enemies of the Jews hoped to gain mastery over them, the *reverse* occurred: the Jews gained mastery over those who hated them" (9:1).

It has ever been like this. In terms of the insight of the New Testament, we know that God's people are often persecuted and despised. Those who follow Christ and belong to him will sometimes face great difficulty (John 15:18–20). In many parts of our world today Christians are suffering and are persecuted, but one day they will be vindicated; one day the reverse will occur. One day God will judge the wicked, and his people will be with him forever. In the book of Esther we see a historical situation anticipating that great reversal at the end of time.

Then I saw a new heaven and a new earth, for the first heaven and the first earth had passed away, and the sea was no more. And I saw the holy city, new Jerusalem, coming down out of heaven from God, prepared as a bride adorned for her husband. And I heard a loud voice from the throne saying, "Behold, the dwelling place of God is with man. He will dwell with them, and they will be his people, and God himself will be with them as their God. He will wipe away every tear from their eyes, and death shall be no more, neither shall there be mourning, nor crying, nor pain anymore, for the former things have passed away." (Revelation 21:1–4)

The Battle Begins

The fighting begins in 9:5, and five hundred men are killed in Susa, along with the named ten sons of Haman (9:6–10). The king reported the news and asked Esther if she had a further request. "Now what is your wish? It shall be granted you. And what further is your request? It shall be fulfilled" (9:12). Esther said, "If it please the king, let the Jews who are in Susa be allowed tomorrow also to do according to this day's edict. And let the ten sons of Haman be hanged on the gallows" (9:13). She wanted their bodies displayed for all to see as a public example.

Esther's Behavior

It may be that Esther's concern was legitimate. It may well be that there is a contrast between the reference in verses 6 and 12 to "Susa the citadel" and Susa more widely. In other words, the enemies of the Jews in the fortified part of Susa had been eradicated, including the ten sons of Haman (who were just as anti-Semitic as their father; so they too got their comeuppance). It may well be that Esther was saying, "I know there are other enemies of the Jews in the town at large, and they have not yet been dealt with." That may have been a legitimate concern, but it also appears that there was a degree of bloodthirstiness in Esther (even though the writer doesn't give any insight into the motivation or even the morality of what is happening here; he just describes it). She was perhaps becoming a bit like the people she lived with.

Her behavior was certainly a long way from the ethical standards of the new covenant taught by Jesus in the Sermon on the Mount about how to treat our enemies (Matthew 5:43ff.). But the large number of enemies that were killed (75,000, 9:16; LXX 15,000) may well reflect the considerable anti-Semitism that the Jews had to suffer in the empire, or perhaps it was an indication of how the Jews' defense had gone too far, given the opportunity, and become simply a rather less-well-controlled "vengeance" (8:13). It is important to remember that it appears only "men" were killed (9:6, 15) in response to the armed attacks against them. Also, the Jews did not take the plunder they were entitled to by the edict (9:10–11, 15), therefore showing restraint (they remembered the dangerous sin of Saul who had taken plunder from the Amalekites against the command of God). It should also be noted that spread across the 127 provinces mentioned in 9:30 (see also 1:1), there were fewer casualties in each province than in Susa itself. However, regarding the decree and its implementation, Alec Motyer comments, "But from this point onwards the book takes a tragic turn. Given the opportunity to write a new edict, cancelling the first, Mordecai turns it into an opportunity for revenge, giving the Judeans permission to slaughter their enemies. . . . Esther herself requests a second day's slaughter."[3]

I recall some years ago being at Yad Vashem in Jerusalem, the memorial to the Holocaust victims, and particularly a series of reflected candles memorializing the large number of Jewish children killed by the Nazis, an incredibly moving display. I was standing behind two young Jewish men about twenty years of age, and one said to the other, "It makes you think doesn't it—that the world could have done this to us. We must never let them do it again." "Yes," said the other Jewish young man, "and isn't it even more amazing that we are now doing that to others." What a sobering comment!

In Esther's day the tables had been wonderfully turned in God's goodness, but we may also be seeing the dark side of Esther. All God's people need his ongoing grace and transformation, and Esther (even though used by God) needed that too. There is sometimes a hair's breadth between justice and revenge. It is definitely right for people who have been sadly abused or who are victims of prejudice to seek justice, but that can easily become a desire for vengeance and sometimes end up unfairly hurting and victimizing others. We also need to remember that while we rightly strive for justice now, it is only on the final day of judgment that perfect justice will be accomplished by God himself.

Esther's Priority Concern

The key point here as we look at Esther's example is her forthrightness driven by her priority concern for the welfare of God's people. This is a key issue, and it raises a question that we need to ask ourselves as we think about the story. Will we do what is right and trust God as Esther did, or will we do what seems best to us in the choices that face us in life? Will we do what we know is right in terms of standing up for what God wants us to do and how God wants us to behave? Will we do what is right and trust God with the consequences, even if our lives are on the line? Or will we do what seems easier and best for us?

Application

That's the kind of issue that faces every man and woman of God—young and old and in between. Young people who belong to the church, are you willing to trust God for the key relationship of your life? Are you willing to trust God to lead you to the right partner, or are you simply going to do what seems best to you at the time? Are you willing to do what you know is right and trust God, or will you try to hurry along God's hand?

At work, others may have to choose between security and job tenure or compromise by being passive about dishonest business practices. As Christians in a world where it is increasingly difficult for believers to hold Biblical ethical standards, will we do what is right, or will we do what seems easiest and best for us?

Esther made commitment to God's people her top priority. She put herself on the line for the health and safety of her fellow Jews. Today, commitment—to our partners, to a job we have put our hands to and need to finish, even to our Savior—is often somewhat inadequate. Too often commitment to God's people is lacking among Christians. Some born-again Christians hold Christian fellowship quite loosely these days. The number of regular church attenders is declining. Of course, there are sometimes legitimate reasons not to be at church on a given Sunday—a sick child, elderly parents who need visiting, an unbelieving partner, and so on. But we do well to ask ourselves regularly, how committed are we to God's people? How committed are we to the worship of God and the health and well-being of the local church to which we belong? Who is going to be the next generation of church elders, deacons, or pastors? Who is going to do the youth work when current leaders have moved on? Who is willing to put themselves on the line for the well-being of God's people? Sometimes we have to admit that we tag on our commitment to God's people and God's church, for which he died, at the end of an otherwise busy week. Certainly as Christian people, we have a responsibility under God to be good husbands or wives, good parents, good members of our family, good people at work. But we must not let those tasks crowd out our commitment to our brothers and sisters in our eternal family with whom we will share Heaven one day. How seriously do we take the health and well-being of God's people, of which we are a part?

Some time ago I read an article by the then bishop of Manchester. It stated in part:

The bishop of Manchester, Nigel McCullock, said the established church was in danger of becoming a minority sect and that, "We will, unless there is a turn in the tide, be a church that gradually disappears from this land." Bishop McCullock went on to say that clergy were being diverted from their true mission of evangelism. "It is almost as if the devil is in this— it distracts people from what they are meant to be doing. Far too many of us are being forced into managing an institution rather than engaging with the souls. The moment that an institution goes down that road it has lost its heart and the purpose for which it was created."[4]

There is no guarantee from God that the Church of England or any other denomination will exist for as long as the world exists. There is indeed a guarantee that his people, the church, will exist forever, but there is no guarantee that any particular denomination will do so.

What about the churches where we are? How serious is our commitment to our brothers and sisters in Christ and the mission to which Christ has called us? The book of Esther raises that very question. Esther was willing to put her life on the line along with her security as the queen of the greatest empire on earth because of her priority commitment to God's people. She was forthright in a great and good cause, for she knew how central the church of God was in his purposes in her day, as the post-Pentecost church is in ours.

I mentioned before that the Lewes District Council had decided to "modernize" by abandoning prayers before council meetings, appointing no chaplain, and having no civic service. One councilor was quoted as saying, "Prayers before council meetings are irrelevant. All prayer is irrelevant." That is but one example of the wholescale attempt today to marginalize or remove the Christian faith from public influence in our schools, governments, and institutions. Western media generally have little respect for the Christian faith, and I would even go so far as to say that the media have a bias against the Christian faith. Will God in his mercy use us to turn the tide?

The Feast of Purim

Esther 9:20ff. relates the establishment of the Feast of Purim. Purim is an interesting play on the word *pur*, which meant the casting of dice or lots. Haman was trying to vent his anger against God's people by annihilating them, planning not only to deal with his one enemy but to wipe out all of Mordecai's people, and he sought some sort of help to accomplish that. Haman, being superstitious, thought the world was influenced by blind chance or fate, so he cast lots. We could say this was like consulting a horoscope, trying to determine the best time to act. But the book of Esther tells us that the events of this world are not the product of forces of chance or fate, but rather of God working out his purposes to redeem, keep, and look after his people. He will bring them safely through the problems of this world; they are secure in him. Our lives are not under blind forces of chance but rather under God's gracious ruling and protecting hand.

Deliverance Celebrated

When we look at this great reversal, when God's people were due to be annihilated and it seemed that nothing could save them, we see that they were actually delivered by God. That's the key theme of the book of Esther—God's deliverance. Comments from Gordon McConville are helpful:

> It is God's reliability in the cause of his faithful people which is the narrative of the book of Esther. . . . The central thing for the Jews then, as believers now, is that God does not ultimately abandon his people to the tender mercies of fortune, or of wicked men, but rules and overrules for the well-being of his people.[5]

The faithful, promise-keeping God delivered his people.

> And Mordecai recorded these things and sent letters to all the Jews who were in all the provinces of King Ahasuerus, both near and far, obliging them to keep the fourteenth day of the month Adar and also the fifteenth day of the same, year by year, as the days on which the Jews got relief from their enemies, and as the month that had been turned for them from sorrow into gladness and from mourning into a holiday; that they should make them days of feasting and gladness, days for sending gifts of food to one another and gifts to the poor. (9:20–22)

What great days of joy and feasting that first celebration must have been! The Jews committed themselves to celebrate this festival "throughout every generation, in every clan, province, and city" (9:27–28).

Mordecai and Queen Esther were now powerful in their positions of influence and wise in how they handled the king, giving him as much credit as they could for his actions (9:25). It is interesting to note that Esther grew in confidence the more she stood up for and identified with God and his people (e.g., 9:13, 32). The first time we take courage in our hands and witness for Christ is always the hardest, but it becomes easier the more we do it.

God's people had been delivered, and they were to be reminded year by year of God's goodness to them and how he brought about their "relief and deliverance" (4:14). Celebration was encouraged and enjoyed. They were to have a celebration for two days of feasting and gladness to remember God's deliverance, and Purim was to be added to the other great Mosaic feasts in the Jewish calendar. Jews celebrate Purim to this day, with a day of fasting and prayer and a day of great celebration along with the reading of the book of Esther, accompanied by boos when Haman appears and cheers when Mordecai is mentioned.

New Testament Application

As we turn to the pages of the New Testament, we see that the deliverance in Esther's day was simply a foretaste of the greater deliverance won for you and me by the Son of God at great cost on the cross. There he faced evil head-on, and was victorious. He gave his life rather than take revenge against his enemies and laid down his own life as a sin-bearing substitute for us, that we might be forgiven. Jesus' resurrection opened the gateway of Heaven for us. His resurrection was the vindication of all that he said and did on our behalf. The New Testament people of God are meant to be a people who are constantly feasting and rejoicing because of what Jesus has done for us. Jesus our Savior has given us a meal to help us do that, a foretaste of the feast and joy of Heaven, as we remember constantly in Holy Communion his love to us—his body broken and blood shed so that we might be forgiven and have eternal life. How thankful we should be!

You and I, like the people of God of old, our forefathers, need to keep remembering how good God is to his people, how much he can be trusted even when it seems as if he is far away. Reminders of God's particular goodness to us, memory markers of special times or events, can also be helpful. The book of Esther teaches us that the hidden hand of providence is always at work. God is with us, even when we don't feel his presence. How good and faithful he is to his people!

As we think of great David's greater Son who overcame evil to bring us eternal life, and as we rejoice in the resurrection of Jesus, we are meant to be people of joy who, as we meet together, anticipate the feast and delight of Heaven itself. We are meant to be people who delight to sing our Savior's praise.

Concluding Challenges

Esther challenges us in three ways. Firstly, are we willing to get our priorities right in terms of commitment to God's cause and God's people? Secondly, are we longing for a reversal in the so-called "fortune" of the church in our day and our generation? Thirdly, are we willing under God's hand to play our part in that?

At the foot of the cross let us remember just how great the deliverance is that God has won for us, how great an answer that is to the deepest questions of the human heart, how secure a place it is to be. Do we doubt that we are loved? Are we insecure about our future? Why should we do anything else but trust him, anything but want to obey and follow him? In him we are loved and eternally secure.

May God grant that the challenges and the truths of these chapters come home to us with new force in lives recommitted to Christ and to his people. May we experience renewed joy and renewed confidence, trusting God for all our todays and tomorrows.

Although I hope that you have seen that I have been basically sympathetic to Mordecai and Esther in their unique historical situation, though willing to be critical where I think necessary, not all Jewish or Christian commentators are as kind. For example: "In sum, neither Esther nor Mordecai nor the Jews show love for God or for their neighbors, the identifying marks of the true covenant people of God."[6] The Apocryphal text of Esther also, which came much later than the canonical version, shows by its scribal additions what some Jews felt was missing from the godliness of Mordecai and Esther.[7] But this is sadly to miss the subtlety of the original author and what he is trying to say so brilliantly.

The Conclusion of Esther

ESTHER 10

AS CHAPTER 10 IS ONLY three verses long, I will make some comments not only about this chapter but about the book generally.

New governments, whatever their election promises may be, generally increase taxes. Mordecai was now the new prime minster, but the burden of tax still needed to be paid (10:1). God's people were not delivered from the ordinary demands of life.

The book of Esther is history told as story and displays plenty of historical verification. The mention of Persian customs and the decorations of the royal palace at Susa as well as the axe-wielding soldiers around the king show that the writer was familiar with the royal court (we know about these from excavations at one of Xerxes' other palaces at Persepolis and subsequent displays at the Louvre in Paris, as well as Persian decree details from the Cyrus Cylinder in the British Museum). The character of Xerxes and the historical setting as described by Herodotus fit well with the six months of feasting in Susa in 483 B.C. and the despondent return of the king after the defeat of his navy at Salamis in 480 B.C. The fact that secular records mention a Marduka, probably Mordecai (a Hebraized form of the Babylonian name Marduka) as a key royal official at the time is the icing on the cake (10:2, 3).

Mordecai is remembered by a wonderful epithet: "he was great among the Jews and popular with the multitude of his brothers, for he sought the welfare of his people and spoke peace [*shalom*] to all his people" (10:3). He was a good and popular prime minister, just as he had been a valuable palace official. He looked out for the good and well-being of the church of his day and sought additionally to be a peacemaker. Being concerned for the welfare of the church is not hostile to the blessing of a whole society. In fact, quite the opposite is true. We need more politicians with that sort of concern for their people and their nation in government today.

Esther 9:20–32 has already explained the historical origin of the yearly Jewish Feast of Purim (a play on the word *pur*, or dice), at which the book of Esther is read in full, accompanied by pantomime-style boos and cheers for the goodies and baddies. The feast celebrates God's sovereign deliverance of and commitment to his people and his steadfast love for them. Throughout the book God's rule, though often hidden, is seen to be both loving and personal. The events of the world are not the result of blind fate or chance as Haman thought.

The brilliant way in which the story is told, its careful structure and parallels, not to mention its comic and dramatic irony (and sarcasm), make it a compelling read. It is ideally suited to be an extended acted parable. It may be that the author's use of some names is comically symbolic too, as Ahasuerus (the Biblical name for Xerxes), when said in Hebrew, sounds like "king headache."

Some Final Thoughts on Esther

The Key Question of the Book

We must not miss the key question that this book answers. For the Jews at the time, whose sin had brought them into exile as God had warned, and especially for those who after the return from exile had remained for whatever reason in Persia, the key question was, "Will God still keep his covenant commitment to us while we are away from his special presence and the fulfillment of his promises in Jerusalem/Judah? Is he still with us in this pagan world? Can we trust him when he seems so absent from us and we still have to cope with pagan rule?"

The wonderful answer this book gives us is that God always keeps his promises, that he can and should be completely trusted, and that, as Paul would later state it in terms of the new covenant, "I am sure that neither death nor life, nor angels nor rulers, nor things present nor things to come, nor powers, nor height nor depth, nor anything else in all creation, will be able to separate us from the love of God in Christ Jesus our Lord" (Romans 8:38–39). Geography can't separate us from God's love; our failures can't; even death itself can't! As Jesus put it, "I am with you always, to the end of the age" (Matthew 28:20). Ultimately, we will be with him forever, face-to-face, in his Father's house (John 14:1–3).

We need to apply this truth to the post-Christian or pagan situations we may find ourselves in today as those who belong to the Lord's family, exiles from our heavenly home (Philippians 3:20–21). Is God with us in the office, at school, on Monday mornings, even when he seems far away compared with the joy and fellowship of worshiping with God's people on the Lord's Day? He most certainly is! Even when it doesn't seem to be the case, his providential care for his people is working behind the scenes and throughout history to save, keep, bless, and bring to Heaven a people for his glory, those his beloved Son has redeemed. God's agenda remains and is always the "relief and deliverance" (4:14) of his elect in Christ.

Will We Trust God's Providence?

This is the key application of the book of Esther.

Will we trust God when nothing seems to be happening (much is), when it seems contrary to self-interest? Will we be obedient to his revealed Word and trust him, knowing he knows what is best for us? Will we identify with God's people and trust him for the consequences? Will we believe that God is sovereignly ruling and overruling for good in our lives (cf. Romans 8:28; Ephesians 1:22–23)? Will we trust that God's agenda is always the "relief and deliverance" (4:14) of his people?

Gordon McConville's comment bears repeating, as it sums up very well what we have been considering: "It is His reliability in the cause of His faithful people that constitutes the real point of the narrative."[1]

God is utterly reliable and can be totally trusted! Karen Jobes also helpfully highlights the importance of providence in the book:

> The major theological point of the book of Esther is that God fulfills his covenant promises through his providence. The major point of contemporary significance is that God unfolds his will for individual lives through that same providence. God continues to work through providence, through seemingly insignificant events, to call people in every age to himself. . . . He uses the ordinary events of life, some happy, some quite tragic, to form Christ in us.[2]

That should lead us, as she rightly says, "to ponder the miraculous quality of the ordinary. As it has been said, 'a coincidence is a miracle in which God prefers to remain anonymous.'"[3]

The wonderful truth for the Christian is that because of all that Jesus has done for us as our Lord and Savior—all that it cost him to leave Heaven, be born as a man, and go to the cross for us—it is unthinkable that he would ever fail us in life or in death. We can be completely confident that his love for his faithful people can be trusted whenever and whatever we face. As King David put it, "The steadfast love of God endures all the day. . . . I trust in the steadfast love of God forever and ever" (Psalm 52:1, 8).

Soli Deo gloria!

A Select Bibliography

EZRA, NEHEMIAH, ESTHER

*OUTSTANDINGLY HELPFUL
**BRILLIANT

General Introductory Books

Baldwin, Joyce G. "Esther." In *The New Bible Commentary*. 21st Century Edition. Leicester, UK and Downers Grove, IL: InterVarsity Press, 1994.

Herodotus. *The Histories*. Translated by Robin Waterfield. Oxford, UK: Oxford University Press, 1998.

Longman III, Tremper and Raymond Dillard, eds. *An Introduction to the Old Testament*. Grand Rapids, MI: Zondervan, 2006.

Merrill, Eugene H., ed. *Ezra—Song of Songs*. The Bible Knowledge Word Study. Colorado Springs: Victor, 2007.

*Motyer, J. Alec. *Roots—Let the Old Testament Speak*. Fearn, Scotland: Christian Focus, 2009.

*Waltke, Bruce K. (with Charles Yu). *An Old Testament Theology*. Grand Rapids, MI: Zondervan, 2007.

Williamson, H. G. M. "Ezra and Nehemiah." In *The New Bible Commentary*. 21st Century Edition. Leicester, UK and Downers Grove, IL: InterVarsity Press, 1994.

Wright, J. Stafford. "Ezra and Nehemiah." In *The Biblical Expositor*. Edited by Carl F. H. Henry. Nashville, TN: Holman, 1974.

Commentaries

Adam, Peter. *Ezra and Nehemiah*. Reading the Bible Today Series. London: Aquila Press, 2014.

Allen, L. and T. Laniak. *Ezra and Nehemiah*. New International Biblical Commentary. Peabody, MA: Hendrickson, 2003.

Baldwin, Joyce G. *Esther*. Tyndale Old Testament Commentaries. Downers Grove, IL: InterVarsity Press, 1984.

Bechtel, Carol M. *Esther, Interpretation*. A Bible Commentary for Teaching and Preaching. Louisville: John Knox Press, 2002.

Boice, James Montgomery. *Nehemiah: An Expositional Commentary*. Grand Rapids, MI: Baker, 2005.

Breneman, Mervin. *Ezra, Nehemiah, Esther*. New American Commentary. Nashville, TN: Broadman & Holman, 1993.

Brown, Raymond. *The Message of Nehemiah*. Bible Speaks Today. Downers Grove, IL: InterVarsity Press, 1998.

Davis, Dale Ralph. *Ezra and Nehemiah*. This material was originally published in the online magazine *Thirdmill* and can still be accessed online at https://thirdmill.org /magazine/.

*Duguid, Iain M. *Esther and Ruth*. Reformed Expository Commentary. Phillipsburg, NJ: P&R, 2005.

ESV Expository Commentary. Vol. 4. *Ezra—Job*. Contributions from W. Brian Aucker and Eric Ortlund. Wheaton, IL: Crossway, 2020.

Fensham, F. Charles. *The Books of Ezra and Nehemiah*. Grand Rapids, MI: Eerdmans, 1982.

**Jobes, Karen H. *Esther*. NIV Application Commentary. Grand Rapids, MI: Zondervan, 1999.

*Jobes, Karen H. and Janet Nygren. *Esther*. Bringing the Bible to Life. Grand Rapids, MI: Zondervan, 2008.

Kaiser, Walter C., Jr. *Revive Us Again*. Fearn, Scotland: Christian Focus, 2001.

*Kidner, Derek. *Ezra and Nehemiah*. Tyndale Old Testament Commentaries. Downers Grove, IL: InterVarsity Press, 1979.

Lamb, Jonathan. *Nehemiah—Faith in the Face of Danger*. Keswick, UK: Keswick Ministries, 2004.

*McConville, J. G. *Ezra, Nehemiah and Esther*. Daily Study Bible. Philadelphia, PA: Westminster Press, 1985.

Nielson K. and D. A. Carson. *A Study in Nehemiah*. The Gospel Coalition. Nashville: Lifeway Press, 2014.

*Packer, J. I. *A Passion for Faithfulness: Wisdom from the Book of Nehemiah*. Wheaton, IL: Crossway Books, 1995.

Phillips, Elaine. *Esther*. The Expositors Bible Commentary Revised. Grand Rapids, MI: Zondervan, 2010.

Rata, Tiberius. *Ezra and Nehemiah*. A Mentor Commentary. Fearn, Scotland: Christian Focus, 2010.

Reid, Debra. *Esther*. Tyndale Old Testament Commentaries. Downers Grove, IL: InterVarsity Press, 2008.

*Reynolds, Adrian. *Teaching Ezra*. Fearn, Scotland: Christian Focus, 2018.

Roberts, Mark. *Ezra, Nehemiah, Esther*. Mastering the Old Testament. Nashville: Word, 1993.

*Shepherd, David J. and Christopher J. H. Wright. *Ezra and Nehemiah*. The Two Horizons Old Testament Commentary. Grand Rapids, MI: Eerdmans, 2018.

Swindoll, Charles R. *Esther*. Nashville: Word, 1997.

*Thomas, Derek W. H. *Ezra and Nehemiah*. Reformed Expository Commentary. Phillipsburg, NJ: P&R, 2016.

Webb, Barry G. *Five Festal Garments*. New Studies in Biblical Theology, No. 10. New York: Apollos, 2000.

Williams, Paul. *Ezra—The Lord Helps*. La Grange, KY: 10 Publishing, 2020.

Williamson, H. G. M. *Ezra, Nehemiah*. Word Biblical Commentary. Nashville: Thomas Nelson, 1985.

Yamauchi, Edwin M. *Ezra and Nehemiah*. Grand Rapids, MI: Zondervan, 2010.

Notes

Chapter One: Our God Reigns—See God
  1. Bruce Waltke (with Charles Yu), *An Old Testament Theology* (Grand Rapids, MI: Zondervan, 2007), p. 774.

Chapter Two: The Church Family Matters—See the Church
  1. J. Stafford Wright, "Ezra and Nehemiah," in *The Biblical Expositor*, ed. Carl F. H. Henry (Nashville, TN: Holman, 1974), p. 359.

Chapter Three: First Things First—Returning to Worship
  1. Philip Paul Bliss, "Man of Sorrows, What a Name" (1875), www.hymnary.org.
  2. John Samuel Bewley Monsell, "O Worship the Lord in the Beauty of Holiness" (1863), www.hymnary.org.

Chapter Four: Facing the Battle
  1. Derek Kidner, *Ezra and Nehemiah*, Tyndale Old Testament Commentaries (Downers Grove, IL: InterVarsity Press, 1979), p. 49.

Chapter Five: The Temple Finished and Dedicated
  1. Eugene H. Merrill, ed., *Ezra—Song of Songs*, The Bible Knowledge Word Study (Colorado Springs: Victor, 2007), p. 56.

Chapter Six: "Lord, Please Do It Again"
  1. J. Stafford Wright, "Ezra and Nehemiah," in *The Biblical Expositor* (Nashville, TN: Holman, 1974), p. 363; and following him, H. G. M. Williamson, *Ezra, Nehemiah*, Word Biblical Commentary (Nashville, TN: Thomas Nelson, 1985), p. 100.

Chapter Seven: Believers Face Challenges
  1. "We Are Marching in the Light of God," first verse is a South African traditional, translated by Anders Nyberg. Copyright © 1984 Peace of Music Publishing, administered in the USA by Walton Music Corp., a division of GIA Publications Inc., and in the UK by Wild Goose Publications. Reproduced by permission. The second and third verses are by Andrew Maries. Copyright © 1987 Sovereign Music UK. Used by permission sovereignmusic@aol.com.

Chapter Eight: The Danger of Dilution
  1. F. Charles Fensham, *The Books of Ezra and Nehemiah* (Grand Rapids, MI: Eerdmans 1982), p. 125.

2. F. C. Holmberg, quoted in Mervin Breneman, *Ezra, Nehemiah, Esther*, New American Commentary (Nashville, TN: Broadman & Holman, 1993), p. 149.

3. L. Allen and T. Laniak, *Ezra and Nehemiah*, New International Biblical Commentary (Peabody, MA: Hendrickson, 2003), pp. 75–76.

4. Breneman, *Ezra, Nehemiah, Esther*, p. 153.

5. Derek Kidner, *Ezra and Nehemiah*, Tyndale Old Testament Commentaries (Downers Grove, IL: InterVarsity Press, 1979), p. 68.

Chapter Nine: Holiness Matters

1. H. G. M. Williamson, "Ezra and Nehemiah," in *The New Bible Commentary*, 21st Century ed. (Leicester, UK and Downers Grove, IL: InterVarsity Press, 1994), p. 431.

2. Joyce G. Baldwin, *Haggai, Zechariah, Malachi*, Tyndale Old Testament Commentaries (Downers Grove, IL: InterVarsity Press, 1972), p. 213.

3. J. Stafford Wright, "Ezra and Nehemiah," in *The Biblical Expositor* (Nashville: Holman, 1974), p. 365.

Chapter Ten: A Good Heart for God and His Work

1. J. I. Packer, *A Passion for Faithfulness: Wisdom from the Book of Nehemiah* (Wheaton, IL: Crossway, 1995), p. xi.

2. David Jackman, teaching at a Proclamation Trust Preachers workshop (London, c. 1995).

3. Raymond Brown, *The Message of Nehemiah*, Bible Speaks Today (Downers Grove, IL: InterVarsity Press, 1998), p. 32.

4. Richard Lovelace, *The Dynamics of Spiritual Life* (Downers Grove, IL: InterVarsity Press, 1979), p. 160.

5. Joseph Scriven, "What a Friend We Have in Jesus" (1855), www.hymnary.org.

6. Eugene H Merrill, ed., *Ezra—Song of Songs*, The Bible Knowledge Word Study (Colorado Springs: Victor, 2007), p. 68.

7. Brown, *The Message of Nehemiah*, p. 34.

Chapter Eleven: Making the Most of the Opportunity

1. J. Alec Motyer, *Roots: Let the Old Testament Speak* (Fearn, Scotland: Christian Focus, 2009), p. 358.

Chapter Twelve: Sharing the Vision and Starting the Work

1. Raymond Brown, *The Message of Nehemiah*, Bible Speaks Today (Downers Grove, IL: InterVarsity Press, 1998), pp. 26–27.

2. This selection was taken from J. I. Packer, *A Passion for Faithfulness: Wisdom from the Book of Nehemiah* (Wheaton, IL: Crossway, 1995), pp. 96–98. Used by permission of Crossway, a publishing ministry of Good News Publishers. All rights reserved.

3. Packer, *A Passion for Faithfulness*, p. 98.

Chapter Thirteen: The Family of God at Work

1. Derek Kidner, *Ezra and Nehemiah*, Tyndale Old Testament Commentaries (Downers Grove, IL: InterVarsity Press, 1979), p. 84.

2. ESV 2016 footnote.

3. Kidner, *Ezra and Nehemiah*, p. 86.

Chapter Fourteen: Getting the Work Completed

1. Derek Kidner, *Ezra and Nehemiah*, Tyndale Old Testament Commentaries (Downers Grove, IL: InterVarsity Press, 1979), p. 103.

2. Eugene H. Merrill, ed., *Ezra—Song of Songs*, Bible Knowledge Word Study (Colorado Springs: Victor, 2007), p. 78.

Chapter Fifteen: The Importance of Continuity

1. See further explanation by Derek W. H. Thomas, *Ezra and Nehemiah*, Reformed Expository Commentary (Philipsburg, NJ: P&R, 2016), p. 313.

Chapter Sixteen: Revival

1. Walter C. Kaiser Jr., *Revive Us Again* (Fearn, Scotland: Christian Focus, 2001), p. 164.

2. J. I. Packer, *A Passion for Faithfulness: Wisdom from the Book of Nehemiah* (Wheaton, IL: Crossway 1995), p. 153.

Chapter Seventeen: Recounting the Goodness of God

1. D. Martyn Lloyd-Jones, quoted in *Reformation and Revival* 13, no. 3, p. 173.

Chapter Eighteen: Renewing the Covenant

1. Bruce K. Waltke, *Genesis: A Commentary* (Grand Rapids, MI: Zondervan, 2001), p. 146.

2. The Methodist Covenant Prayer, accessed January 4, 2021, https://www.methodist .org.uk/about-us/the-methodist-church/what-is-distinctive-about-methodism/a -covenant-with-god/.

Chapter Nineteen: Recreating Community

1. J. Stafford Wright, "Ezra and Nehemiah," in *The Biblical Expositor*, ed. Carl F. H. Henry (London: Holman Company, 1974), p. 372.

2. Wright, "Ezra and Nehemiah," p. 372.

Chapter Twenty: A Joyful Celebration and a New Beginning

1. Eugene H. Merrill, ed., *Ezra—Song of Songs*, Bible Knowledge Word Study (Colorado Springs: Victor, 2007), p. 92. See also H. G. M. Williamson, *Ezra, Nehemiah*, Word Biblical Commentary (Nashville, TN: Thomas Nelson, 1985), p. 365.

2. Derek Kidner, *Ezra and Nehemiah*, Tyndale Old Testament Commentaries (Downers Grove, IL: InterVarsity Press, 1979), p. 123; see also Kidner's helpful comparison of the lists in Nehemiah on page 122.

3. Merrill, *Ezra—Song of Songs*, pp. 92–93.

Chapter Twenty-One: Broken Promises

1. Gene A. Getz, *Nehemiah*, Bible Knowledge Commentary Old Testament, ed. John Walvoord and Roy B. Zuck (Colorado Springs: David C. Cook, 1983), p. 695.

2. Eugene H. Merrill, ed., *Ezra—Song of Songs*, Bible Knowledge Word Study (Colorado Springs: Victor, 2007), p. 95.

3. *Matthew Henry's Commentary* (Peabody, MA: Hendrickson, 1991), p. 865.

4. H. G. M. Williamson, "Ezra and Nehemiah," in *The New Bible Commentary*, 21st Century ed. (Leicester, UK and Downers Grove, IL: InterVarsity Press, 1994), p. 441.

5. A quote from Motyer's commendation of Derek W. H. Thomas, *Ezra and Nehemiah* (Phillipsburg, PA: P&R, 2016).

6. Derek Kidner, *Ezra and Nehemiah*, Tyndale Old Testament Commentaries (Downers Grove, IL: InterVarsity Press, 1979), p. 130.

7. J. A. Motyer, *Roots: Let the Old Testament Speak* (Fearn, Scotland: Christian Focus, 2009), p. 364.

8. James Montgomery Boice, *Nehemiah: An Expository Commentary* (Grand Rapids, MI: Baker, 1990), p. 10.

9. Charles Swindoll, quoted in J. I. Packer, *A Passion for Faithfulness: Wisdom from the Book of Nehemiah* (Wheaton, IL: Crossway, 1995), p. 81.

10. Raymond Brown, *The Message of Nehemiah*, Bible Speaks Today (Downers Grove, IL: InterVarsity Press, 1998), pp. 26–27.

11. Kidner, *Ezra and Nehemiah*, p. 89.

12. N. Shaxson, "Out There Amongst the Hills" in *CSSM Chorus Book 1 & 2* (London), www.wakementrust.org.

13. Rev. William Gilbert Jones, "Wounded for Me," verse 1, www.hymnary.org.

Chapter Twenty-Two: The Selection of Esther as Queen

1. J. G. McConville, *Ezra, Nehemiah and Esther*, Daily Study Bible (Philadelphia, PA: Westminster Press, 1985), p. 153.

2. Barry G. Webb, *Five Festal Garments*, New Studies in Biblical Theology, No. 10 (New York: Apollos, 2000), p. 131.

3. Karen Jobes, *Esther*, NIV Application Commentary (Grand Rapids, MI: Zondervan, 1999), 38.

4. J. I. Packer and Derek Williams, *The Bible Application Handbook* (Guildford, UK: Eagle, 2001), p. 98.

5. Joyce Baldwin, *Esther*, Tyndale Old Testament Commentaries (Downers Grove, IL; InterVarsity Press, 1984), p. 21.

6. Jobes, *Esther*, p. 96.

7. Jon D. Levenson, *Esther: A Commentary* (Louisville, KY: Westminster John Knox, 1997), p. 19

8. Jobes, *Esther*, p. 233.

Chapter Twenty-Three: The Plot to Destroy the Jews

1. Bruce K. Waltke (with Chrles Yu), *An Old Testament Theology* (Grand Rapids, MI: Zondervan, 2007), p. 769.

2. Waltke, *An Old Testament Theology*, p. 767.

3. Joyce G. Baldwin, *Esther*, Tyndale Old Testament Commentaries (Downers Grove, IL: InterVarsity Press, 1984), p. 75.

4. Karen Jobes, *Esther*, NIV Application Commentary (Grand Rapids, MI: Zondervan, 1999), p. 136.

5. J. G. McConville, *Ezra, Nehemiah and Esther*, Daily Study Bible (Philadelphia, PA: Westminster Press, 1985), p. 172.

Chapter Twenty-Four: The Reversal of "Fortune" Begins

1. George Duffield, "Stand Up, Stand Up for Jesus" (1858), www.hymnary.org.
2. Paul Williams, *Ezra—The Lord Helps* (Leyland, UK: 10 of Those, 2020), p. 30.

Chapter Twenty-Five: Deliverance for the Jews

1. See the support for this interpretation by Joyce G. Baldwin, *Esther*, Tyndale Old Testament Commentaries (Downers Grove, IL: InterVarsity Press, 1984), pp. 97–98, contra Karen H. Jobes, *Esther*, NIV Application Commentary (Grand Rapids, MI: Zondervan, 1999), pp. 180–81.
2. J. G. McConville, *Ezra, Nehemiah and Esther*, Daily Study Bible (Philadelphia, PA: Westminster Press, 1985), p. 193.
3. Alec Motyer, *Roots: Let the Old Testament Speak* (Fearn, Scotland: Christian Focus, 2009), p. 370.
4. Ruth Gledhill, "Bishop Warns Church That It May Disappear," *Times*, March 20, 2004, https:// www .the times .co .uk /article /bishop -warns -church -that -it -may -disappear-bzng8sz7p0j.
5. McConville, *Ezra, Nehemiah and Esther*, p. 190.
6. Bruce K. Waltke (with Charles Yu), *An Old Testament Theology* (Grand Rapids, MI: Zondervan, 2007), p. 768; see also pp. 765–70.
7. English Standard Version Bible with Apocrypha (New York: Oxford University Press, 2009).

Chapter Twenty-Six: The Conclusion of Esther

1. J. G. McConville, *Ezra, Nehemiah and Esther*, Daily Study Bible (Philadelphia, PA: Westminster Press, 1985), p. 190.
2. Karen Jobes, *Esther*, NIV Application Commentary (Grand Rapids, MI: Zondervan, 1999), p. 46.
3. Jobes, *Esther*, p. 233.

Scripture Index

General Index

Aaronic-Zadokite line of high priests, 49
Abraham, 26, 129, 162
Agag, 156, 157
Ahasuerus, 146, 156
Amalekites, 156, 158
anti-Semitism, 151
Aquila, 127
Artaxerxes, 20, 39, 42; as impressed with Ezra's learning and lifestyle, 50
Ashdodites, 94

Babylonia, 27
Baruch, 90
Battle of Salamis, 146
Bible ministry, 53
Bliss, Philip Paul, 36
Book of the Law, 108
Breneman, Mervin, 63
Brown, Raymond, 74, 83
Bunyan, John, 57

Christianity, 40
Christians, 44, 74, 166; and the flaunting of their faith, 151; freedom of to express Christian values, 164; marginalization of, 180; obedience as fundamental to, 61; the role of Christian leaders, 62
Church, the, 136, 163; and the discovery that obedience brings joy, 109–11; gathering of, 108; and the high regard for Scripture, 108; importance of in God's purposes, 28–29; need of for faithful preachers, 109; in the Two-Thirds World, 20; in the West, 19–20. *See also* Church, the, continuity needed in; world, the, in the Church

Church, the, continuity needed in: continuity in doctrine, 104; continuity in fellowship, 104; continuity in worship, 104
Church of England, 185
Cyrus, 20, 21, 22, 23, 39, 42, 43, 73–74
Cyrus Cylinder, the, 22

Darius, 20, 39, 42, 43, 146
David, 25, 33, 129–30, 169
Day of Pentecost, 66
divorce, 67
Duffield, George, 166
Dunkirk (2017), 39
Dynamics of Spiritual Life, The (Lovelace), 75

Eareckson, Joni, 43
Egypt, 50, 116
ekklesia, 108
Esther (book and person of), 143–45; application of Esther to God's people, 175–76; application of Esther to God's rule, 175; behavior of, 182–83; choice of, 177–78; commitment of to God's people, 184; concern of, 178; concluding challenges concerning, 187–88; courage of, 165–67, 177; on a domestic situation made worse by legislation, 148–49; importance of God's providence in, 144; hiddenness of God in, 144–45; historical background of, 145–46; as history told as a story, 189; irony in, 146–47; key questions concerning the book of, 190–91; as more than an explanation of Purim, 144; New Testament application, 187;

Index of Sermon
Illustrations

Community
We must recognize even today the importance of continuity and the community of believers, 103–5

Faith
We must understand the difficulty of maintaining our faith, 97

God's Goodness
Nehemiah's recounting of the goodness of God should remind us of God's continuing faithfulness to believers, 115–19

God's Presence
We must face the difficult question of whether God is near or far away in our everyday lives, 143–44

God's Purposes
We must recognize that the world continues and will continue to bring opposition to the purposes of God, 41–42

Jerusalem
Jerusalem central to the purposes of God in the Old Testament, 74

Jesus Christ
Jesus is the embodiment of grace and truth in our lives and an example to us all, 68

Leadership
The leadership examples of both Ezra and Nehemiah are relevant to Christian leadership today, 49, 53, 65, 67–68, 137–38

Obedience
The discovery within the Church that our obedience as believers will bring us joy, 109–11

People of God
We must recognize and acknowledge the types of persons God uses for his purposes, 51–52

Prayer
The personal prayers of Ezra as an example for our own prayers, 62–63
The prayer of Nehemiah as a guide to our own prayers (confession, conviction, and praying to the God of the covenant), 75–78

Providence
The providence and care of God for his people throughout history, 23, 171–72, 191–92
Esther presents the coincidences of providence, 169

Redemption
God's working through history to achieve the purpose of redemption, 21–22
The providential provisions of God for his people's redemption last even to today, 23

The Preaching the Word series is written
by pastors for pastors and their churches.

crossway.org/preachingtheword